I loved this book. Kate brings a
with hope and light to times of
hugely helpful and humorous
devotional reading to be dry an

Professo   *.......... ....,*
author and motivational speaker

This book is a much-needed daily dose of good news! Kate's honesty, insight, humour and lived experience will encourage you to trust God in every circumstance. Highly recommended!

Cathy Madavan, author and speaker

Life doesn't always flow the way we think it will. It can feel like disappointment, frustration and despair. Especially when we feel God has led us onto a pathway he set us on, and our minds begin to try to understand and ask the hard questions such as why is life not going our way? What went wrong? Did I not hear God correctly? Then the 'But God' can begin to bring a fresh outlook on the situations that have impacted us.

Through Kate's refreshing honesty and personal reflections on her own journey she unpacks the possibility of 'But God' in her own challenges and disappointments. She very cleverly draws out and explores the deeper work that God is doing in the background in our lives. Kate brings hope from her very real experiences encouraging us to look beyond, enabling you as the reader to glimpse the bigger picture being revealed. A book to be read, be meditated on and walked out in the face of challenge.

Alison Fenning, speaker, evangelist and
co-founder of Mission on the Move

I love the real-life feel of this great devotional book. Kate has brilliantly fused the Bible and life together giving it a light but meaningful tone. The teaching and reflections are well thought through landing with honest but faith-filled prayers. You will be blessed as you engage.

Revd Mark Greenwood, national evangelist and head of evangelism at Elim Churches UK

Kate's writing and insights are a refreshing hit to the daily devotional world – she bypasses cliché and mundane thoughts and brings out fresh takes on ancient Scriptures. I found myself laughing out loud (actually 'lol'ing) as she authentically unpacks how God's power is with us in our ordinary, everyday moments. Kate's humour and down-to-earth thinking make this devotional so fun and deeply encouraging. I will genuinely be recommending this to people as it is quite simply brilliant.

Rich Martin, key relationship lead at Glorify, podcaster, richmartin.co.uk

If you want a straight to the point, funny, yet powerful guide to life – this is it! It hit the spot and spoke into my life where I didn't know I needed it – that's the mark of an outstanding book. Kate is a gifted writer who brings life-changing guidance and insight with ease, helping you see that what you are going through is easier to deal with than you realised. Hope-filled, faith-filled and reality-filled – this is the book that will change how you see life and all it brings your way.

Vicky Cross, lead pastor at Relentless Church, Warrington

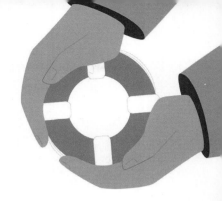

WHEN GOD 'BUTS' IN

FINDING STRENGTH
TO FACE THE IMPOSSIBLE

KATE WILLIAMS

Authentic

First published 2023 by Authentic Media Limited,
PO Box 6326, Bletchley, Milton Keynes, MK1 9GG.
authenticmedia.co.uk

British Library Cataloguing in Publication Data
A catalogue record for this book is available from the British Library.
ISBN: 978-1-78893-308-7
978-1-78893-309-4 (e-book)

Cover design by Wonderburg

Printed and bound by CPI Group (UK) Ltd, Croydon, CR0 4YY

DEDICATION

This book is dedicated to Gwen.

Gwen – I want to thank you for your example of being a person of true faith, joy and trust in the face of some very challenging circumstances. Your walk of faith has given me great hope that it's possible to go through difficult times and still maintain a tenacious spirit, quick wit, a deep level of trust in Jesus and a cheeky twinkle in your eye.

You are an amazing lady who has imparted so much into so many people's lives. You are much loved and will be very much missed here. I look forward to a 'knit and natter' with you again one day in our heavenly home. Please save me a seat by you and a big piece of cake.

Kate xx

Gwen Kirby (1927–2022)

ACKNOWLEDGEMENTS

First of all, I want to thank my husband, Rod – as without him it's fair to say this devotional would not have been published! Rod – thank you for believing in me and encouraging me to approach Authentic Media with my first book. I know you are very much looking forward to the sequel, *When Rod Butts In* – and I'll certainly have lots of material for that one! I appreciate your love, support, encouragement and advice throughout this process very much.

Big thanks to the team at Authentic Media who have been lovely to work with. I am impressed with how prayerful they are throughout the process and the family feel they bring to working with them. I greatly appreciate the opportunity they have given me to get my first book out there.

Thank you to my lovely mum who has encouraged me in my writing, and who was a huge support through the challenges of our fostering process. Thank you for always being there for advice, wisdom and care – I love you lots.

Thanks to my good pals, Hannah and Ros, who read the very early manuscript and encouraged me to make it into a book for others to read. Ros – our writing days together have been a blessing – I look forward to your book being published one day soon (that's a hint to get on with it!).

Thank you to Adele at Harmony House in York for hosting me on my writing retreats. Couldn't ask for a better host or a nicer place to get away to write and be refreshed. I highly recommend Harmony House as a peaceful escape to help the inspiration flow.

I also recommend everything on the breakfast menu as I'm pretty sure I've now sampled all options.

Thanks to Carl and Lisa for always encouraging me in my writing, and for your honest and helpful feedback throughout the process. Love you guys and really value your friendship.

I'm so grateful to everyone who has taken the time to read and endorse my book. You are all busy people and I don't take for granted your time, feedback and encouragement – it really means a lot.

Paul and Helen McGee – that phone call with you when you were stuck in traffic was such a helpful one (well for me, perhaps not so much for you!). Your advice and wisdom particularly around the title (lol!) has made a massive difference. Paul – thank you for always being so willing to help me with my many queries – and for always responding with weird and wonderful WhatsApp voice notes – I enjoy them very much! The promised curry and a pale ale are defo on the cards for you (but only on a Monday when our local Indian does a good deal, and only if more than three people buy this book – otherwise it's beans on toast and tap water).

I'm thankful to God for inspiring me to write down these thoughts and things I learnt through my own personal challenge. I'm thankful that God is patient as I wrestle with him through the many questions and mysteries on this journey of faith.

Thank you to everyone who has bought this book. I pray it will encourage you and spur you on to keep believing for God to 'but in', especially when you are in the thick of an impossible situation.

Kate x

CONTENTS

PROLOGUE

The phrase to 'butt in' is usually used to describe a negative interruption – when someone is sticking their nose into someone else's business. However, through a challenging time I faced, I learnt the importance of asking God to 'but in' as I studied biblical examples of the incredible power of God when he brings a 'but' into a situation that appears impossible.

When God 'buts in' he isn't meddling or interfering, he is divinely intervening in our situation. I believe we should welcome this – well, more than that, I believe we should long and pray for it to happen. Our attitude should be to say: 'Bring on the divine interruptions – bring on the biblical "but ins"'.

Are you facing a situation that humanly speaking is looking bleak and impossible? I'd love for you to come on a journey with me as I walk you through an obstacle I recently faced in my own life. I wrote a big chunk of this devotional as someone who was in the middle of a challenging time, longing and believing for God to 'but in' and do the impossible. I wanted to look at God's word and his promises and stir my faith, and I also want the same for you in whatever seemingly impossible situation you are facing.

Sometimes when God 'buts in' we experience a miraculous turnaround in our situation. Sometimes God 'buts in' and gives us peace, patience, confidence, or grace to sustain us through the trial. I believe God wants to 'but in' and be actively involved in our lives – especially when we feel that our situation is hopeless or impossible. I hope that looking at these thirty reflections on biblical 'but ins' stirs your faith and gives you renewed energy to move forward in your challenging time. I'd encourage you to actively ask and believe for God to 'but in', and trust that he knows the intervention you most need.

When I wrote this book, I was facing the very real possibility that a big dream of mine might not be fulfilled. I felt like I was at a crossroads where I could easily become discouraged, angry, frustrated, anxious and stressed – and all with good reason. Instead of responding in fear and anxiety as I so often have done before, I wanted to spend the time while I waited for the outcome looking to God, his word and his wisdom, and actively living in faith and expectation that God would do a miracle and 'but in' with divine help.

In a nutshell, my husband and I were almost at the end of a long process to become foster carers. We are adoptive parents to our beautiful little girl who has Down Syndrome, and while we didn't feel ready to care for another child full time, we felt we could do a bit more in offering respite care. The process to get approved went fairly smoothly and it looked very much like the outcome would be favourable. Then suddenly, what appeared to be a massive mountain was blocking our path. Certain policies had quickly changed, which, because of our personal circumstances, meant it was likely that we would be permanently disqualified from ever becoming foster carers. The sadness and confusion I felt on receiving that news was devastating. Hearing the words 'permanently disqualified' was like being punched in the gut.

But.

Humanly speaking, things may well look bleak and impossible. But. It's a three-letter word that can make a huge difference. It doesn't deny the problem, but it allows room for the problem not to be the end of the story. 'But' is defined as 'on the contrary', 'yet', 'unless' or 'except that'. 'But' provides an opportunity for a counter point of view to an impossible situation. I believe it is God's 'but ins' that we need to hold on for.

In this devotional I want us to reflect together on some examples of biblical 'but ins' – where believers we read about in the Bible had huge obstacles in their way. But God stepped in. But God showed up. But God did a miracle – and the humanly impossible became possible. I'm naturally not a hyper-positive person. It's an effort for me not to be cynical and not to live feeling swamped by the difficulties I see around me. However, I've been a Christian since I was eight years old, and I really felt it was time to start looking at life from a faith-filled perspective, rather than just accepting what I saw with my natural eyes. I wanted to activate my faith to a level I hadn't lived in previously. To live like I believe God is who he says he is and that he really can do anything. To believe that those Sunday-school stories I often sang about as a child were about miracles that really did happen, and they were not just 'chirpy church choons' with ridiculous actions.

I'm no 'blab it and grab it' prosperity-gospel-type gal. I don't believe God promises to make our lives easy or pain-free, and give us everything we want including our own private jet. Yuck – we'd all be like that horrible Verucca Salt girl from *Charlie and the Chocolate Factory* if that were the case! (Give me an Oompa Loompa any day.) However, instead of only praising God when I look back and see how he has worked with hindsight, I wanted to learn how to thank and praise him and stand in faith for a miracle before it had happened, and when it seemed extremely unlikely to happen. I wanted to activate my faith in the middle of the trial, believing for God to 'but in'.

This book is not some kind of guarantee that God will 'but in' to your situation in exactly the way you'd like him to. You'll see the ups and downs of my situation as you read on, and you'll see from my personal story that things don't always go as we plan or hope for them to. God did some amazing and miraculous things through my personal situation, which I talk about through this book. I have to admit though, that in another circumstance I've recently faced,

God's 'but in' was not a big turnaround miracle, it was the promise that he will make his power perfect through my weakness (which to be truthful cheesed me right off!). I prefer the miraculous turnarounds if I'm honest, but God is God and he 'buts in' as he sees fit!

I don't know what you are facing – it's likely that it's not the same scenario as me. Although our situations may well be very different, I believe we need to stand together in choosing to activate our faith in a God who can do the impossible. To look with fresh eyes at what the Bible says and to shake off the unbelief – perhaps understandably caused by years of despair and disappointment in life.

You may have chosen to read this because you are having serious issues in your marriage or another significant relationship. It could be that you are struggling to conceive and a positive pregnancy test seems increasingly unlikely. Maybe you have been made redundant and are struggling to find work, or you do have a job but you are not flourishing in it and you yearn for that opportunity to develop new skills. Perhaps you or a loved one has received a difficult health diagnosis. There are a whole host of challenges we have to walk through while on this planet. I'm feeling prompted more than ever to try to look at situations through eyes of faith and not fear. I'm reminding myself of God's power, and remembering that he really did do the miracles I've grown up reading about. There's always hope for him to 'but in', whatever struggle we find ourselves in.

If you want to believe for God to 'but in' along with me, please keep reading. If you like big 'buts' and you cannot lie, then I pray you'll be encouraged as you take these next thirty days to reflect on God's truth that helped me immensely in the middle of my impossible situation.

                                                              Kate :)

GOD HAS A STRONG 'BUT'

Against all hope, Abraham in hope believed and so became the father of many nations, just as it had been said to him, 'So shall your offspring be.' Without weakening in his faith, he faced the fact that his body was as good as dead . . . and that Sarah's womb was also dead. Yet he did not waver through unbelief regarding the promise of God, *but* was strengthened in his faith and gave glory to God, being fully persuaded that God had power to do what he had promised. (Romans 4:18–21)

This passage from Romans has always been one I've really loved. It's so challenging, but so helpful when we believe God has spoken yet it looks like it'll never ever happen. God's promise to Abraham was that he would be the father of many nations. This passage makes no secret of the natural obstacles he and Sarah were up against. I really love that the Bible says Abraham was able to face the facts of his situation without weakening his faith. It's possible to hold those two things in tension and to remain in faith. It always cheeses me off when people deny being ill or having difficulties. 'I was healed at the cross, sister' they say while they are red-nosed and sneezing all over you! Go to bed, Rudolf, say a prayer and have a Lemsip for goodness' sake! We don't need to pretend we are not in trouble, but we do need to declare God's promises over our lives and our belief that he can 'but in' and deliver us.

So what was Abraham and Sarah's reality? Abraham's body *was as good as dead* and Sarah's womb was *actually dead*. Talk about bleak and lacking in hope! I can't help but picture a really crusty old couple who I can't believe would even want to 'do the deed' when I think of Abraham and Sarah. His body is as good as dead and her womb *is* dead – it's not exactly painting a picture of saucy, fertile times! I doubt they'd be appearing on any series of *Love Island*. They'd need a stairlift to get in the pool if they did! They might just about manage 'doing it' without dying – if they were lucky!

But . . .

> He [Abraham] did not waver through unbelief regarding the promise of God, **but** was strengthened in his faith . . . being *fully persuaded* that God had the power to do what he had promised.

Wow!

We, like Abraham, can choose to rely on God's strength and increase our faith through our challenges, remaining *fully persuaded* that God holds ultimate power to do what he has promised, regardless of where our crustiness levels lie.

To waver means to become unsteady, to begin to fail or give way, to feel or show doubt and indecision. I believe that wavering happens as we give more time to the facts and realities we see than we do to God's ability to do the impossible. Like I've already explored, we don't need to deny the reality we are facing, but we do need to ensure we don't give it too much power or attention. I could very easily go into waver mode as I reflect on the facts surrounding my situation. Policies have changed. Disqualifications have come into play. The top person who has the final decision is 'very unlikely' to say yes to us. Waver dot com.

But.

The God I worship parted the Red Sea. God raised the dead. God put life into barren wombs. God changed the heart of a powerful Pharaoh. God changed water into wine (and it wasn't that cheap Lambrini I used to buy as a youth – it was the good stuff).

When I reflect on how big and amazing and almighty God is, the wavering largely goes away. However, I feel like it's a daily battle on the wavering front, as I believe we have an enemy who wants us to be distracted, disillusioned and doubting God's power and presence in our situations. He will bombard us with scary realities and things may well even begin to appear worse – I've certainly found that within our situation.

Our circumstances may well look and feel hopeless, human-ly speaking, but let's join with wrinkly old Abraham – against all hope, and in the face of extreme crustiness, to believe God will 'but in' with the breakthrough.

Remember – God always has the final say, and his 'but' can strengthen us in our faith as we wait for him to do the impossible.

REFLECTION

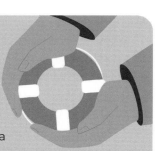

What is the impossible seeming situation you are currently facing?

What issues are involved that make a breakthrough in this situation look humanly impossible?

How are you doing in terms of wavering?

Practically what I have done is write every Scripture, song lyric and encouraging message I have received about our situation on massive sheets of paper in our study. Every day I am reading them out loud and declaring God's reality over my situation – war room-style!

We need to constantly remind ourselves of God's perspective – and in doing so we are strengthened in our faith. Every time you have a discouraging thought, say out loud a promise of God you have received about your situation.

Can you get practical and begin to write down what you feel God is speaking and promising over your situation? (If you do go 'war room-style' like I did, watch out for the blue tack – it can be a pig to get off!)

PRAYER

God, today I thank you for the examples of people in the Bible who modelled great faith. Thank you for Abraham and Sarah, an old and crusty couple who chose to believe in your power to fulfil your promise to them, despite exceptionally bleak natural obstacles. Thank you that, like Abraham, I can 'against all hope, in hope believe' and choose to rely on your strength and ability. Help me not to waver in unbelief as I'm bombarded by the reality around me, but to be firm in my conviction that you are the God who put life into a 'dead' womb. I invite you into the areas of my life that appear hopeless, weak and vulnerable, as I recognise they are the very areas that are no problem for you to work through. Thank you that I can learn, as Abraham did, to be *fully persuaded* that you will keep your promise to me, regardless of what is happening around me. Amen.

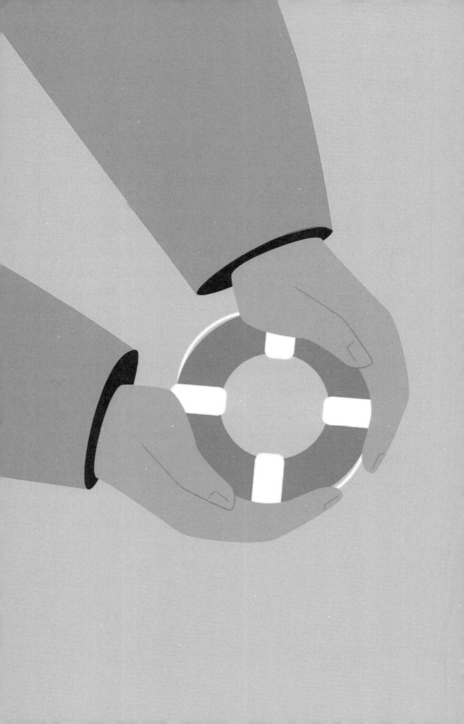

WHEN GOD'S 'BUT' IS PRESENT, ANYTHING IS POSSIBLE

Jesus looked at them intently and said, 'Humanly speaking, it is impossible. *But* not with God. Everything is possible with God.' (Mark 10:27, NLT)

The scenario leading up to Jesus making this incredible statement is an interesting one. A rich man asked Jesus how he could have eternal life. He told Jesus that he had kept all of the commandments since being a boy. Jesus 'looked at him and loved him' (v. 21), then proceeded to challenge him to sell all he had, give it to the poor and follow him. The man walked away sad as he was very wealthy and was unwilling to give up the dollar.

Jesus then told his disciples that it was easier for a camel to fit through the eye of a needle than for a rich person to enter the kingdom of God. In case you are worried that this verse refers to some strange kind of camel-crochet life group Jesus was trying to set up, I'll briefly explain what this reference means. There are two main schools of thought relating to this Scripture. One is that Jesus literally did mean to use a camel and a needle eye as two extremes of large and tiny things, highlighting the impossibility of a camel and the 'fullness of its humpage', if you will, passing through a tiny needle eye. The other theory is that the 'eye of the needle' was a narrow gateway into Jerusalem. Camels and the 'fullness of their humpage', plus the material possessions of a rich person they would be loaded up with, would be a right faff to try to squeeze through the slim gateway. All the expensive goodies would have to be removed before squashing poor old 'Humphry' through the tiny gap, then loading him up with the luxury luggage again on the other side. I've always thought the gate option was more likely, though it is debated as to whether this gate actually did exist. Either way, be it 'camel crochet' or 'camel gate' – it's undoubtedly an exceptionally tricky manoeuvre.

My life with a five-year-old is pretty dominated by 'The Wiggles' (please Google if you are not familiar – but be warned that you may well wonder if you've accidentally taken illegal drugs after watching). I'm very familiar with 'Zamel the camel' and his five humps. I'm well aware that stuffing him through a needle eye is a pretty impossible-seeming task. But Jesus says that it *is* possible for people with great wealth to know him and to enter his kingdom. What seems humanly impossible is actually possible with God. With God, five-humps Zamel can pass through the needle eye.

God wouldn't ask of us things we didn't have the capacity to do. He doesn't set us up to fail. The rich man had a choice. It wasn't impossible for him to enter God's kingdom, but he chose his wealth. I don't say that judgementally, as if I would easily have made a different choice in his shoes (he was wadded so they were probably Jimmy Choos), I'm just highlighting that he had a choice.

We too have a choice. It may feel like getting a breakthrough is less likely than Zamel the ruddy camel (and did I mention his five humps?) getting through the eye of the needle. But Jesus says that all things are possible with God. Will we choose to believe that, or will we have the hump about our situation? (sorry – but to be honest there's much worse to come!)

Saying this, Jesus isn't like a fairy Godmother – as if we can be, do or have anything we want in life because it's all possible in God. Bibbety bobbity boo! It doesn't work like that. We may wish it did sometimes. But we are not in a fairy tale, we are in a spiritual battle. We are also challenged by Jesus, as the rich man was, to 'deny ourselves, take up our cross and follow him' (see Matt. 16:24). In the rich man's case, this denial of self was related to his material wealth. Denying ourselves may look different in our individual circumstances, but it's central to our walk of faith. Authentic Christian faith is not a fluffy 'skipping through fields with Jesus' type of situation. It requires costly sacrifice and obedience on a big scale. But if we do respond to the call of Jesus and sacrifice the things that would hold us back, he will give us favour and we will see impossible things become possible through him.

In terms of the impossible situations we are currently facing, we must ensure that what we are believing for is in God's will. We don't need to stress and get all intense about this. But we need to be sure that God has spoken to us – which he does in many different ways as we are all so unique. One of the main ways he speaks to us is through the Bible. His word is 'alive and active' (Heb. 4:12).

My personal testimony on this front is that a few days ago I decided to get up early and ask God to speak to me about my impossible situation. Sometimes we can think we have heard God or were led by him to do something, and we can be wrong. I remember applying for a *dream* job a few years back and I was convinced God was in it and that I'd get it – and I came extremely close, but then I didn't get it. We can be wrong and that's OK, it's a learning curve. But we need to seek God and ask him what he says about our specific situation. Advice from people close to us who we trust is so important, but above all we must ask God and create space for him to speak to us.

My Bible reading that morning was from the book of Zechariah. I came across a verse I'd never taken note of before but it leapt off the page:

> What are you, mighty mountain? Before Zerubbabel you will become level ground. Then he will bring out the capstone to shouts of 'God bless it! God bless it!'
>
> *Zech. 4:7*

I shared it with my husband and my mum who both agreed it was significant.

Following a very discouraging meeting encouraging us to withdraw from our dream of becoming foster carers, I was scrolling the gram (that means Instagram if you are not young and cool like me) and it suggested a person who is known to have a prophetic gift for me to follow. I'd never heard of him so did a quick stalker scroll through his posts (as you do). A prophetic statement he wrote about mountains caught my eye after reading the verse from Zechariah about mountains being levelled. It said this:

> 'The mountain in front of you is not really a mountain' I heard the Lord say. We are in a time of spiritual games, smoke and mirrors, and facades created to keep your eyes off Jesus and onto problems that don't really exist. These diversions are irrational fears that are prophesying a false future, bombarding discouragement, anticipation of failure, and fear of the times so that you throw in the towel, give up and forfeit being a voice.[1]

The verse directly under this was none other than Zechariah 4:7: 'What are you, mighty mountain? Before Zerubbabel you will become level ground. Then he will bring out the capstone to shouts of "God bless it! God bless it!"'

How kind is God? He really does speak and he will do the same for you. But we must take the time to listen and to seek him and ensure that we have his word over our situation.

The 'capstone' referred to in the verse from Zechariah represents the finishing stone and it's a symbol of completion. The part of the verse that says 'God bless it! God bless it!', in other translations is 'Grace, grace unto it'. This is about God's favour, grace upon grace, God finishing the work he has begun. It will be completed only because of God's grace and with his help. I'll have myself a bit of grace doubled, thank you kindly!

In the chapters to come we will look at some biblical characters who believed in God for the impossible, and we will learn from them how to activate our faith for our own seemingly impossible situations.

P.S. What's the aforementioned Zamel's favourite Christmas carol? 'Oh camel ye faithful'. (You'll grow to enjoy it!)

REFLECTION

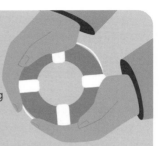

Today I would encourage you to reflect on the words of Jesus relating to our 'but' of the day. 'Humanly speaking, it is impossible. *But . . .* Everything is possible with God.'

When the negative thoughts relating to your impossible situation flood your mind, say these six powerful words, out loud if you can: 'But everything is possible with God.'

Spend some time quietly before God and ask him to speak directly to you about your specific situation.

Think about the rich man in today's Scripture. Is there anything that God might be asking you to give up in order to know him more? A material possession? A habit you know is wrong but are holding onto? A relationship that is no good for you? Remember that God only asks you to give up things that will keep you from knowing him fully and that will prevent you from walking in his calling on your life. He's not a grinchy God who wants to take things from you, he has your very best interests at heart, and wants you to live a full and purposeful life.

Be honest, do you now feel your church is lacking a camel-crochet life group? Maybe you are the perfect person to get one started?

PRAYER

God, thank you for the truth in today's devotion, that all things are possible with you. As my circumstances become more and more impossible-looking, I pray you'll give me more and more belief that you truly can 'but in' and do anything. Challenge me today about anything in my life that, like the rich man and his wealth, is keeping me from walking closely with you. Help me to trust that anything you require me to sacrifice is only because you want me to walk in your perfect plan for my life. I also ask you to speak specifically to me today – please give me a word of confirmation about my situation and show me what your will within it all is. Thank you for the Bible – your powerful, holy word. Draw me to passages that are relevant for me right now and that can guide me as I go forward. I want to cling to your word through this challenging season. You are the God of the impossible. Amen.

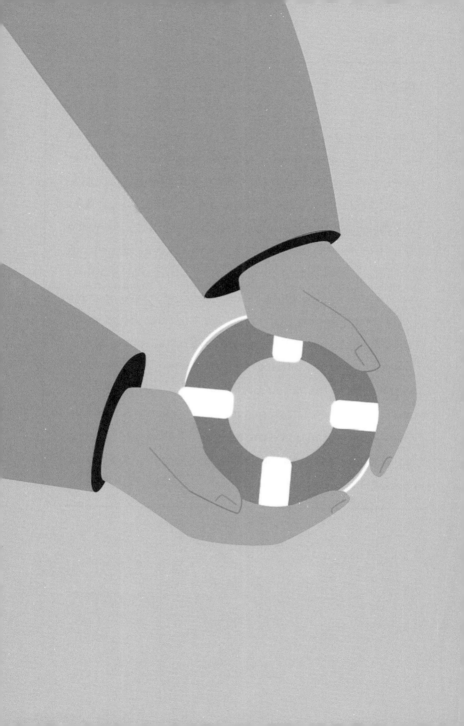

WHAT IF GOD'S 'BUT' DOESN'T SHOW UP?

But even if he does not, we want you to know, Your Majesty, that we will not serve your gods or worship the image of gold you have set up. (Daniel 3:18)

I felt it was important to address this 'but' early on. I recently read the story of Shadrach, Meshach and Abednego (or 'your shack, my shack and a bungalow' – an easy and effective way I was taught to remember their names!) who refused to bow down to false gods, even though they were ordered to do so by King Nebuchadnezzar. (On a very bizarre side note, I once starred in a church play where we named a news-reading character 'Nebuchadtrevor McDonald'. That's strictly copyrighted so don't try and steal it for your next church play.)

Anyway, their punishment if they continued to refuse to bow down would be to be thrown into a blazing furnace. The three men re- spond to the king by saying:

> King Nebuchadnezzar, we do not need to defend ourselves before you in this matter. If we are thrown into the blazing furnace, the God we serve is able to deliver us from it, and from Your Majesty's hand. *But*

even if he does not, we want you to know, Your Majesty, that we will not serve your gods or worship the image of gold you have set up.

Dan. 3:16–18

I greatly admire their confidence, faith and boldness. Even more than that, I admire their willingness to trust God and remain faithful to him regardless of the outcome of their situation. I haven't chosen this 'but' to create a sense of uncertainty around whether God will 'but in' to our circumstances. I've chosen it because I want to declare now that God is more important to me than my dream and receiving my miracle. I'm not denying the pain and confusion involved if at the end of all of this we get told we cannot go forward with what we feel so strongly called to do. It's a huge deal to me, it's one of the few things I've ever felt sure of being called by God to and something I really long to give my time to. If it doesn't happen and if God doesn't supernaturally turn this around, I will be devastated. And that is OK. It's absolutely necessary to grieve and work through disappointment. We shouldn't try to short-cut that. Whatever we face, we go through it with Jesus who has experienced the full range of human emotions to extreme levels. We are never alone.

Again, it comes back to the choices we have. If the mountain isn't moved, will we spit our dummy out, sulk and turn our back on our faith? Or will we dig in, face the hard work of healing and be determined to stay faithful and declare God's goodness anyway? Challenging stuff, not easy at all.

Shadrach, Meshach and Abednego knew God had the power to save them from the blazing furnace. In declaring their 'but' they displayed a huge level of trust in the God who holds the bigger picture. They would give their lives if necessary to honour their God.

The story has an incredible ending. They are thrown into a blazing furnace, and the king is so angry at their disobedience to him that he cranks up the heat so high that the fire kills the people who had to throw them into it. Shadrach, Meshach and Abednego are completely unharmed. The Bible says that they didn't even smell like fire. This was brought home to me as my husband bought me something off eBay recently, which must have been from a seller called 'Fag Ash Lil' – when it arrived and I opened it the smell of cigarettes nearly knocked me over. So to come out of this kind of fire and not to even smell like you've been for a cuppa at Fag Ash Lil's is a huge miracle in itself!

When the king looked on he saw a fourth person in the furnace with them who looked like 'a son of the gods'. What an incredible miracle! God protected them perfectly in the middle of a blazing hot furnace. God can 'but in' and do the impossible. God can reverse natural laws. God can stand with you in a fire and ensure you are completely unharmed. *But even if he doesn't* . . . what will our response be?

REFLECTION

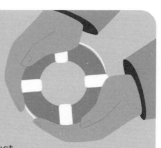

Think about Shadrach, Meshach
and Abednego and their attitude
of immense trust in this situation.
Have an honest conversation with
God about where you are at with trust.

If God doesn't 'but in' and give you a miracle, how will you
feel? Do you feel able to continue to love and trust him regardless of the outcome of this situation you are praying
about?

Have you ever had a 'Fag Ash Lil' style eBay experience? I
once had an epic Amazon fail – I spent £10 on a very styl-
ish (!) garden gnome and when it arrived it was the size of
a matchbox. Gnome delivery gone wrong!

PRAYER

God, today I ask for your help to choose to continue to serve you and believe you are good, regardless of the outcome of my impossible circumstances. Thank you for the incredible display of trust from these three men in today's passage. I want to learn from them and grow in trust, knowing that you are a good God who wants the best for me. I want to honour you as they did, being confident that you are able to 'but in' and totally change things, but humble to accept that you know best if this doesn't change and I don't get my breakthrough. It's so challenging, God, as I'm desperate for you to answer and turn my situation around. Help me as I wrestle with this difficult area of submission to your will. Help me to decide now to love and serve you wholeheartedly, regardless of what happens with the miracle I am asking you for. Amen.

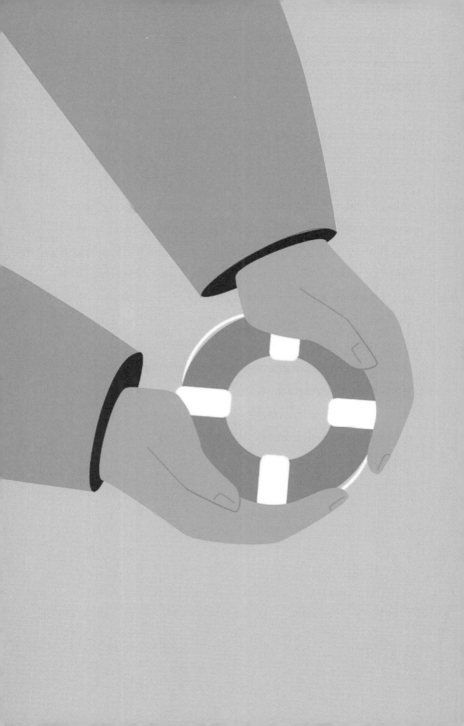

GOD'S 'BUT' CARRIES PEACE

I have told you these things, so that in me you may have peace. In this world you will have trouble. *But* take heart! I have overcome the world. (John 16:33)

Peace is a wonderful gift from God. His peace is such a supernatural thing and I'm so grateful that he offers it to us, especially in the troubling times we face. True and lasting peace is only found in him.

My situation is humanly causing me feelings of stress, anxiety, frustration and anger. I am daily (and at times hourly) having to choose to give the situation back to God and to refuse to allow it to rob me of my joy and peace. It was my birthday this week and I received an email concerning our situation that caused me and my husband to feel stressed and angry. We talked it through and then I said I felt we needed to pray and then choose to leave it with God. We resolved not to think or talk about it anymore that day (not wanting to waste good cake-scoffing time on worrying!). So that's what we did. We had peace – and a big piece of birthday cake! Since then we've done things to further address the email.

Sometimes we don't have the luxury of time, and action is needed there and then. But often, where possible, letting some time pass, even just a day or so, before acting or responding is wise. It means we don't react irrationally and we can carefully and prayerfully consider our next steps. But in the meantime, and in the middle of the mess, I believe we can still live in peace.

There's a degree to which I believe we have to choose peace. If we sincerely go to God and tell him we desire to live in peace despite the panic surrounding us, he will be faithful and offer us that peace. It's always there for us to tap into. But we must continually choose to live and walk in his peace, despite what we see with our natural eyes. We must consistently choose peace over panic.

Peace is powerful, not passive. Peace is not about pretending our problems don't exist, or denying the difficulty we are experiencing.

Peace is confidence in God's ability to handle your situation and it expresses itself through calmness and stillness in your spirit and demeanour. People around you may wonder how you are managing to stay so calm, but his peace is supernatural – it goes way beyond our human understanding. It doesn't make logical sense, as naturally speaking most of us are prone to panic under pressure.

These verses from Philippians are amazing to cling to right now:

> Do not be anxious about anything, but in every situation, by prayer and petition, with thanksgiving, present your requests to God. And the peace of God, which transcends all understanding, will guard your hearts and minds in Christ Jesus.
>
> *Phil. 4:6–7*

I *love* this! It reminds us that God stations his bodyguard of peace at the door of our hearts and minds to deter doubt, fear and anxiety from invading us. I like to think of an Arnold Schwarzenegger-type figure (my personal peace police!) standing by my heart and brain ready to kick butt on any negative and anxious thoughts! Say 'If your name's not peace you're not coming in' out loud in your best Arnie accent! Tell any doubts to peace off! (I hope that joke goes over my grandma's head.) If Arnie doesn't float your boat, think of an alternative personal peace police bodyguard for yourself.

A couple of nights ago everything relating to my situation was buzzing in my brain and I found it difficult to switch off and sleep. So, I started to speak out loud that Jesus is in control. I spoke out the Scriptures I believe he has highlighted to us. And it wasn't long before I drifted off. Many times before I have not done that and have remained overwhelmed by problems. But I'm learning that peace is powerful – I'm choosing to receive it and to live in it as much as I possibly can. Every time a thought or circumstance tries to throw you off, enlist the help of your peace police bodyguards and remind yourself of who God is, what he has done and what he has promised he will do.

Jesus has overcome and he will overcome again and again in the battles we face. In the Scripture we opened with today, Jesus tells us to 'take heart' in troubling times. To take heart means to be of good cheer, to be confident and courageous.

As we face our impossible situations let's do our best to be courageous, and to live with his supernatural peace.

REFLECTION

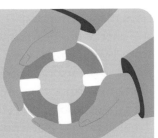

How much peace do you currently have in your impossible situation?

Are you really stressed and wound up, or have you been able to give it to God and leave it with him?

What is one thing you could do today to choose peace? Here's a few suggestions if you are stuck:

1. Say the Scripture from Philippians 4:6–7 every time you feel panic setting in.
2. Listen to an Enya track in front of a candle while stroking some foliage (!)
3. Choose to focus on the bigness of God, rather than focusing on the many complications and obstacles in your situation.
4. Pray for peace – this is my 'choosing peace' prayer. Write your own or use the one on the next page if it helps:

_____

_____

_____

_____

_____

PRAYER

God, this circumstance is really hard, victory seems impossible and it looks like everything is stacked against me. I'm being bombarded with negative circumstances, thoughts and realities. But you say that with you all things are possible. With you, seas were parted and mountains can be moved. So I bring to you all of my doubts, fears, anxieties and struggles. I stop trying to reason and figure it out myself. My job is to stand firm, to be at peace and trust you. Your job is to do miracles and so I choose to receive your peace, to walk in it and to do my best to say 'No' to every anxious thought that pops into my mind. I set my hope and confidence in you and I do not allow this issue, as big and daunting as it may appear, to take away my peace. I take heart, because you have overcome. Amen.

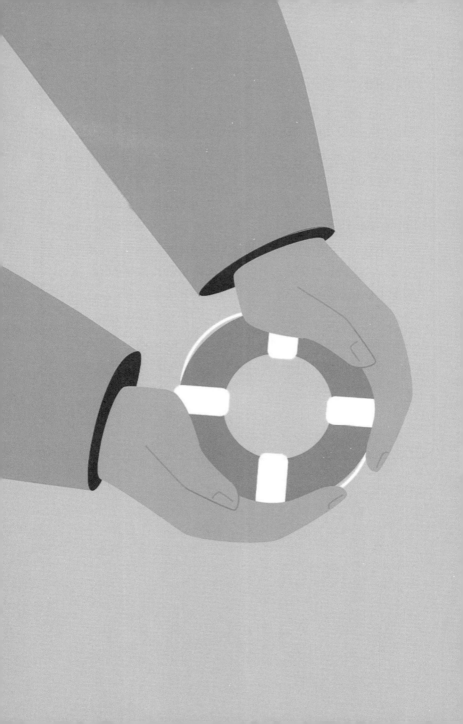

LOOKING AT GOD'S 'BUT' BRINGS HEAVEN'S PERSPECTIVE

We do not know what to do, *but* our eyes are on you.
(2 Chronicles 20:12)

This morning I read in 2 Chronicles 20 about an incredible story of God's power to win a battle. It involves a king called Jehoshaphat. He hears that an army is advancing against him and his people. The Bible says he is alarmed by this, yet he resolves to inquire of God for his perspective on the situation.

God answers by saying that he himself will fight the battle, that they should stand firm in their position, not be discouraged or afraid because the battle is his, not theirs. 'You will not have to fight this battle. Take up your positions; stand firm and see the deliverance the LORD will give you' (v. 17).

Jehoshaphat encourages the people saying; 'Have faith in the LORD your God and you will be upheld' (v. 20). Then Jehoshaphat sends out his army and he appoints people to sing praise to God as they march into battle – they walk towards the enemy singing, 'Give thanks to the LORD, for his love endures for ever' (v. 21). Singing may sound like a pretty weird strategy – a (Jehosha)phat lot of good that will do, you might think! But as they praise and worship God in this way, look at what God does:

> As they began to sing and praise, the LORD set ambushes against the men of Ammon and Moab and Mount Seir who were invading Judah, and they were defeated.
>
> *2 Chr. 20:22*

It's another incredible Bible passage that can lift our faith levels. It seemed that Jehoshaphat and his people were at a massive disadvantage. The enemy were already on their way and they had little warning. They weren't prepared. But rather than crumble under this bad and frightening news, Jehoshaphat is honest in saying he doesn't know what to do, but he turns his eyes to God who he knows will have the answer.

There is great power in praise. God is always worthy of our praise and he loves it when we express our love for him in words, prayers and songs. Praise also brings a sense of God's perspective. When we praise, our focus shifts from the doom and gloom, enemies and impossibilities. When we declare that God can make a way and do the impossible, and how great and mighty he is, we stand taller. We think and talk differently about our situations.

Today's devotion got me thinking about how we are only really expected to sing in times of victory. Taking football as an example, some of the chants highlight this point really well:

> 'You only sing when you're winning.'
> 'It's all gone quiet over there.'
> 'You're not singing anymore.'

I know very little about football. I had a brief interest in Liverpool FC in my youth – the sole reason being that I had a major crush on

Michael Owen. I attended one match at Anfield and have to admit that when I wasn't staring at Michael Owen's legs, I did note that the atmosphere was incredible. Standing shoulder to shoulder cheering, chanting and singing for your team was a great experience. However, the world of football (and sport in general) demonstrates how easy it is to only pipe up with praise and enthusiastic songs when things are going your way. Jehoshaphat shows a different strategy. He instructs the people to sing when it looks like winning is the last thing on the cards for them.

I am finding praising and worshipping in song to be a key factor in my personal battle. Yesterday a couple of small things happened that made me wobble a bit. A friend had sent me a link to the song 'See a Victory' by Elevation Worship. I played it several times and it really helped me to shift my perspective from the earthly situation, to heaven's viewpoint. Faith begins to stir in us again when we sing praise to God and declare his goodness and his truth over our lives and circumstances.

As well as confessing Scriptures, I'm finding singing out and praising God through these biblical truths in songs like 'See a Victory' to be very helpful. In doing so, we keep our faith strong and our sense of God's perspective at the forefront of our minds.

I can relate to how Jehoshaphat felt – 'We do not know what to do.' I know in my own situation there is actually nothing else I can do. But I must switch my perspective to be in line with heaven's perspective, stand firm in my position, sing my heart out and trust God to 'but in' and fight this battle on my behalf.

'We do not know what to do, *but* our eyes are on you.' Let's keep our eyes on God, let's look out for his 'but in' and ask him for heaven's perspective on our battles.

REFLECTION

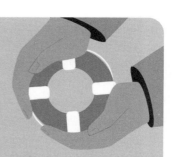

Read the story of Paul and Silas in prison in Acts 16:16–40, and see how praising God impacted their situation. God 'buts in' big time!

Do you feel similar to me, in that you are at a point with your challenge where you are not in control and there's not much more you can personally do to influence things? Choose a praise-and-worship song and praise God through it today. We may not be in control, but we can praise and align ourselves with the one who is.

Here's my suggestion for a 'Pipe up with Praise' playlist – these songs really helped me to praise my way through my situation:

- 'See a Victory' – Elevation Worship
- 'There's Nothing that Our God Can't Do' – Passion Music
- 'Sovereign over Us' – Vineyard Worship
- 'Way Maker' – Bethel Music

A random song but very good (and one you can shake your butt to!): 'When Jesus Says Yes Nobody Can Say No' – Michelle Williams featuring Beyoncé and Kelly Rowland.

PRAYER

God, I can really relate to Jehoshaphat when he says, 'We do not know what to do.' It reflects how I feel – weak and helpless to do anything to change this situation. I want to walk through this experience living out the next few words that Jehoshaphat says: '*but* our eyes are on you.' God, I choose today to fix my eyes and my focus on you. I choose to worship through this challenge, like Jehoshaphat and his army did. I acknowledge that worship is my greatest weapon and it affects the spiritual atmosphere. I will sing to you, my amazing God – you are worthy of all praise and glory. As I sing out your truth, I'm excited to see how you will move in my situation. Amen.

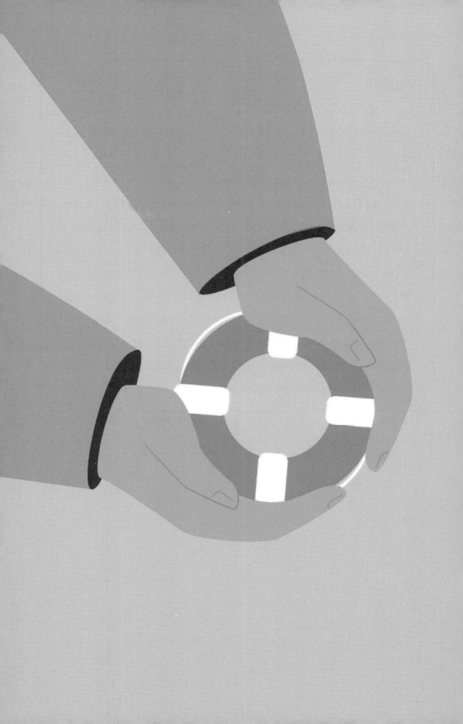

WE CAN BE CONFIDENT IN GOD'S 'BUT'

But I come against you in the name of the LORD Almighty, the God of the armies of Israel, whom you have defied.
(1 Samuel 17:45)

David and Goliath. Shepherd Boy vs. Giant. What an amazing story of one of the most unlikely of victories. This young shepherd boy rocks up to deliver some cheese butties (that means 'sandwiches' – in case you aren't from the North of England) for his brothers. Maybe he was the original 'UberEats' employee? He may well have been riding bareback on a sheep to deliver tasty goods. Ubersheep? Did somebody say Just Sheep? DeliverEwe? I'll stop (for now!). Anyway, David comes on a simple errand to deliver cheese butties and ends up taking on a giant wielding a huge sword, and kills him with a sling and stone. The unlikely victory came about because David wasn't fazed by his enemy – not because the enemy wasn't a serious threat, but because of David's unshakable confidence in God.

What an inspiration to us, as we look at the huge Goliath-like obstacles that are in our way. We can understandably be terrified and doubt that our enemy can fall. Or we can remember God's faithfulness displayed all through the Bible and through our own lives, and stand in confidence that no enemy is a match for Almighty God.

David sees Goliath and confidence rises up in him to defeat this giant. He reflects on his experiences as a shepherd, fighting off bears and lions and knowing God's protection over him. 'The LORD who rescued me from the paw of the lion and the paw of the bear will rescue me from the hand of this Philistine' (1 Sam. 17:37).

As I reflect on my own life I know that God has previously spoken clearly to me, moved supernaturally and made a way for dreams to be fulfilled. At this point of needing another miracle, I'm taking confidence in the fact that I've seen God 'but in' before and I'm believing he can and will do it again. David's confidence in God had grown over years and each new enemy required a new level of confidence in God's power.

I love how David places his confidence in God and not in his own strength and ability. He defeats Goliath, but declares that the glory goes to God:

> You come against me with sword and spear and javelin, but I come against you in the name of the LORD Almighty, the God of the armies of Israel, whom you have defied . . . All those gathered here will know that it is not by sword or spear that the LORD saves; for the battle is the LORD's, and he will give all of you into our hands.
>
> *1 Sam. 17:45–7*

The battle is the Lord's. Your enemy may look gigantic and all geared up with every weapon needed to win. But you and me, like David, can come against the enemy in the name of Almighty God. The name that is more powerful than any gobby, arrogant giant we may face. We need to understand the power in the name of our God, and allow that to fill us with confidence.

Look at what David had – it wasn't much. But in God's hand, a little can be a lot. Every little helps (that's either from the Bible or it's a British supermarket strapline – I can't quite remember which!). Don't look at your life, your circumstances, your bank balance, your giftings or your perceived lack thereof. Build your *character*. God can take the little you have and turn it into something power-ful enough to slay a giant – because he is with you and because he can turn your 'little' into incredible giant-bashing abilities.

Confidence means that you have full trust in someone or some-thing. You totally trust in their power and reliability, which in turn heavily impacts your behaviour and attitude when you come up against a challenge. Imagine what could happen if you operated in full trust – being absolutely convinced that God is on your side and that he will bring you victory.

Confidence can be loud, and confidence can be quiet. I believe confidence can look like staring a giant in the face and declar-ing out loud that God will give you the victory. I also believe con-fidence can be seen in a quiet and restful heart, when circum-stances would naturally cause panic and unrest. Confidence may look different in our various battles, but it must be present, and it must be in God and in his ability, not ours. And when he 'buts in' and brings the victory, we must declare, as David did, that God has won the battle.

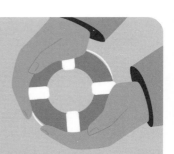

REFLECTION

What does Godly confidence look like in your personal impossible situation? Loud or quiet – or a mixture of both?

What lessons can you take from David's example of standing in confidence in God before a powerful giant when you are armed only with a sling and some stones?

Does reflecting on the past and remembering what God has done in your life previously – as David did – help you in the face of your current giant?

When victory comes, make sure that you follow David's example of giving all the glory to God for helping you to defeat the giant in your life.

What other supermarket straplines could be found in this Bible story? I'm thinking M&S – 'These are not just any cheese sandwiches, these are "strength to slay a gobby giant" cheese sandwiches' (has to be said in sultry tones for it to work). Or Aldi – 'spend a little, sling a lot'? For any American readers – David was certainly well on 'Target' with his sling and stone!

PRAYER

God, I really desire to grow in confidence in you. I'm so encouraged by the example of David, and how all of his shepherding experience led to him having the confidence to take on Goliath. I thank you for every experience I've been through previously that has helped to prepare me for this current challenge I'm facing. I recognise that I need to focus on growing to be a person of godly character, and I embrace the lessons I can learn within this situation that mean I can become more like you. Help me to remember that I have you, the living God, on my side – and because of that I can have great confidence, regardless of the size of the giant in front of me. God, take the equivalent of my little – my cheese sandwiches and my sling and stones – and use them for your glory. Amen.

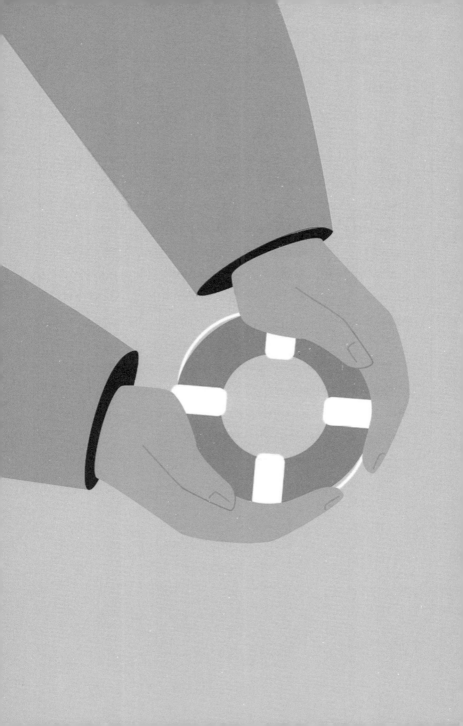

GOD'S 'BUT' IS CONCERNED WITH YOUR HEART, NOT YOUR HEIGHT

But the Lord said to Samuel, 'Do not look at his appearance or his height, for I have rejected him. The Lord does not look at the things people look at. People look at the outward appearance, *but* the Lord looks at the heart.' (1 Samuel 16:7. Double 'but' day!)

Today's first 'but' is a bit of a rewind from yesterday's 'but'. Yesterday we looked at how God's 'but' brought David great confidence in the face of Goliath, the gobby giant. Today I want us to examine an earlier biblical 'but' which allowed David to slay said giant several years later.

Our opening Scripture for today from 1 Samuel describes part of the process of Samuel anointing God's chosen king, which, as you probably know, ended up being the sling-swinging, cheese buttie-bringing Davey baby. One very interesting point in today's passage is that seven of David's brothers were brought before the prophet Samuel as their father Jesse expected one of them to be the next king. Even Samuel himself, a very godly and discerning man, expected the same. He took one look at Eliab and thought, 'He's got to be the one.' God spoke clearly to Samuel and said,

'That's actually not the case.' Samuel and Jesse were focused on the outward – which of the brothers looked beefy, tall, impressive and might rock the royal robe the best. Who would look the most 'in the zone on the throne' if you will! God, however, has a completely different agenda when choosing people for his purposes.

I take great encouragement from the fact that David was not even considered by his earthly father, yet his Heavenly Father certainly didn't forget about him. I love the fact that David was just getting on with the task at hand – busy out in the fields shepherding his sheep, perhaps with no idea what was going on back home. What a fab-ewe-lous example to us of cracking on with our current calling and trusting God to 'but in' and bring change when the time is right.

How do you feel as you are waiting on God in your impossible situation today? Do you feel overlooked, forgotten, invisible? Unskilled, unattractive, not as gifted or talented as you perceive others around you to be? I have certainly felt all the feels of all those things. On days when I am tempted to feel angry at God for not intervening yet, or I'm tempted to compare myself to others and have myself a pity party, I'm encouraged by these words from David's story: 'People look at the outward appearance, *but* the LORD looks at the heart.'

This needs to be my focus – working on my heart and my character as I wait on God to 'but in'. Not looking at others around me and comparing what God's doing for and in them and becoming bitter. God knows me, God sees me. At the right time he will pick me out of the sheep pen, but until then there's plenty to be learnt.

Sheep do a lot of bleating – we can also do too much bleating at times, so let's resolve to 'defeat the bleat' today. It's so important to be talking openly with trusted people about how we are feeling. But it's easy to move from sharing and offloading into bleating mode. Follow my deep advice – 'If you keep repeating, you're probably bleating'! Yes, get things off your chest, ask for prayer and support. But don't keep rehearsing the problems over and over. I know that continually talking about my situation is not good – it robs me of precious time with the people around me in the present moment. It's a huge effort for me not to be consumed by this issue as it's such a big deal, but I must be careful not to repeat and bleat.

Let's speak life and hope over our impossible circumstances. Let's reflect on this story from David's life and be greatly encouraged that, when God is ready, the sheep can shuffle out of the way for us to receive our promise. It's important to note here, said sheep may not be permanently removed. For example, in my situation I'll have more sheep to care for if we can proceed with the dream, it'll mean more responsibility, not a crane lifting me out of a sheep pen and into a spa! Baaaaa humbug.

Samuel asks Jesse if he has any other sons. Jesse says, 'Yes, there's one more who is looking after the sheep.' In rolls David, and he ends up getting anointed as king. One minute he smells of sheep poo and musty wool, the next he smells of the oil of royalty. From sheep rustler to royal hustler (I'm on fire today, I know). I truly believe this turnaround was because David's heart was good. He worked hard, he cracked on, he didn't bleat, he was thankful. God does not over-look a heart like that. It doesn't matter if no one else on the plan-et affirms, believes in, sees or acknowledges you, you are in God's heart. And he cannot resist responding to a heart that is after him.

Today, I want to encourage you to forget about your height, your appearance, your achievements or your lack thereof. Check your heart. Ask God to highlight things you need to work on. Get your head down, do the hard work, keep a good and thankful attitude. Develop a faith and trust in God like David had. Focus your ener-gies on your heart and your character – and let your heart leap looking after your sheep.

I should have a Ewe tube channel. All's wool that ends wool.

REFLECTION

How do you feel about your
circumstances in light of what
God did in the situation we've
considered today? Do you believe
that, as with David, God will not forget
or overlook you even if everyone else does?

Are you sharing with trusted people how you feel, and
have you crossed the line to bleating about it?

Think about your current responsibilities. In what ways
could you be determined to give them your all as David did,
taking great care over the current place God has you in?

PRAYER

God, I ask you to give me a nudge if I'm bleating. This situation is such a big deal to me, and I need to share it with trusted people who can encourage me. But I'm open to you showing me if I'm becoming obsessed with it and if I've crossed into bleat mode. Help me to get the balance right and, if needed, to defeat the bleat. Thank you that when David was cracking on with his shepherding assignment, he kept a good heart and gleaned all he could from that experience. Today I acknowledge that even if no one on the planet has me at the top of their list, you will never ever forget me. Help me to keep on with my current assignment, to knuckle down, have a good heart and remember that if you want to 'but in' and pull me out for other purposes, you are more than able. Help me not to get swept along with the things that our culture says are important – wealth, success, beauty – but to remember that what's important is my heart. I want to have a heart that makes you proud. Amen.

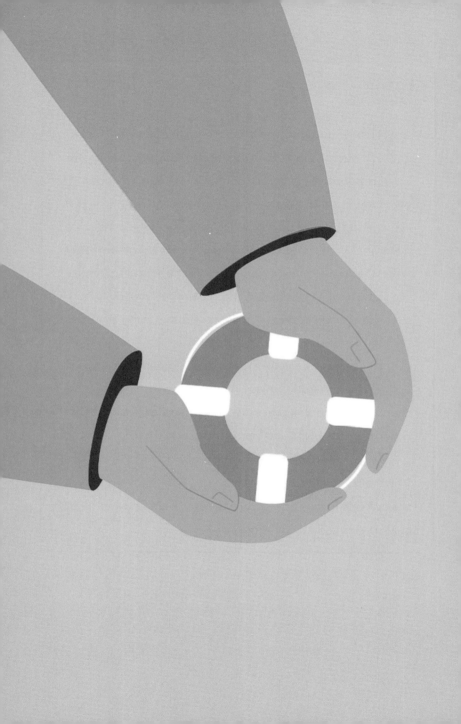

GOD'S 'BUT' IS UNFILTERED

'*Abba*, Father,' he said, 'everything is possible for you. Take this cup from me. Yet not what I will, *but* what you will.'
(Mark 14:36)

I've recently started watching the series called *The Chosen* and it has really helped to bring the Bible to life for me. I think the actor cast as Jesus was such a good choice, and I love the way the writers have included humour, banter and affection between Jesus and his followers. I also love how Jesus has middle eastern features and an appropriate skin colour too – I can't bear the white, pointy-nosed, blue-eyed Jesus portrayed in many historical paintings and films.

Knowing Jesus really helps to keep me grounded in this difficult situation I'm experiencing. I love how the Bible makes it clear that Jesus faced the full spectrum of human emotions. He is a friend and saviour who truly identifies with us in our struggles. He knows first-hand how challenging life on this planet can be. Jesus was let down by close friends and betrayed by one of his inner circle. He faced grief, abandonment, mocking, suffering, anguish and a painful death. He also experienced hunger and tiredness, and was falsely accused of being a drunk. If Jesus had an Instagram account, I don't believe his posts would have been filtered. We wouldn't see him post a face-tuned selfie (complete with a pointy-nose filter!) alongside his disciples with #squadgoals underneath – when the reality is that Peter has just denied him and he knows the rest of them will desert him and let him down. Jesus lived a real and authentic life.

I believe God is interested in what is real, raw and genuine. He wants unedited, unfiltered followers. People who are honest about where they are at, and look to him for help, guidance and trans-formation. I believe we need to be careful during this vulnerable time about how much we engage in the world of social media. I'm certainly not against it, but when you are in a challenging time, it can be especially unhelpful to look at other people's seemingly perfect lives. I also recognise that I can be tempted to post things that make it look as though it's 'all good in the hood', when that really isn't the case. I remember one occasion we were on holiday in Wales and I had a row with my husband. We hadn't even sorted out our disagreement, and yet I took a picture of him in the sun and posted it. It was a good picture, but not a true picture – any-one looking at it would have thought, 'Ah they are having a lovely day', but actually, that wasn't the case at all. I'm not advocating that we post depressing things either – we don't need to share with the world everything that's difficult in our lives to tick the box of being real. But perhaps now is a good opportunity to assess how much time and attention we are giving to the online world and if it is benefiting us or hindering us, particularly during a deli-cate and vulnerable period in our lives.

Jesus is not a filtered God who is aloof, unrelatable and detached from reality. He is a God who became fully human, who under-stands our weaknesses and struggles – who chose to identify with us in our frailty and humanity. He gets it. And he wants to walk alongside us through it. Perhaps in your impossible situation you feel betrayed, left out, invisible, hurt, fed up, anxious, fearful. Take it all to Jesus who *truly* knows how you are feeling. Jesus prayed that God would take the suffering he would soon experience away from him. He ends his emotive prayer by saying, 'Yet not what I will, but what you will.' Jesus trusted that whatever the outcome, God was in control and had plans for good. He knew true submission to his Father because of the deep trust he had in his character. Jesus prayed unfiltered prayers in his time of deep anguish and I believe we should do the same.

REFLECTION

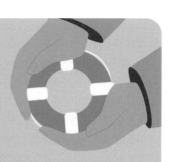

How much are you trusting God
with your situation today? Can you
honestly pray, 'Yet not what I will
but what you will'? Whatever your
answer is, make sure it's unfiltered.

Spend some time reflecting on the emotions Jesus experienced throughout his life and thank him that he is a
friend and saviour who truly understands your pain.

How is your use of social media impacting you during this
time of struggle? Decide on whether you need to take
some time out or if you need to put any boundaries in
place relating to your use of it.

Can you think of a time when you posted something on
social media that in honesty was not a true reflection
of the actual experience? Why do we so often feel the
pressure to prove we are having a great time even if that's
not the case? How can your own social media be more
authentic and unfiltered?

PRAYER

God, I'm so moved by Jesus' submission to you and to your plan, even though he knew it would involve an incomprehensible level of suffering. Thank you for the unedited, unfiltered glimpses you give us into the life of Jesus and the disciples. They experienced the full range of human emotions as we do – joy, pain, anger, awe, disappointment, grief, despair, wonder. Thank you that we have a God who fully understands our humanity, and who can totally identify with the struggles and pain we face. Please help me to evaluate my use of social media at this time, I'm open to you prompting me on whether this needs to be cut back. Submitting to your will is not easy, I may not fully be ready for that today in honesty, but help me to take steps towards genuinely being able to submit to you. Amen.

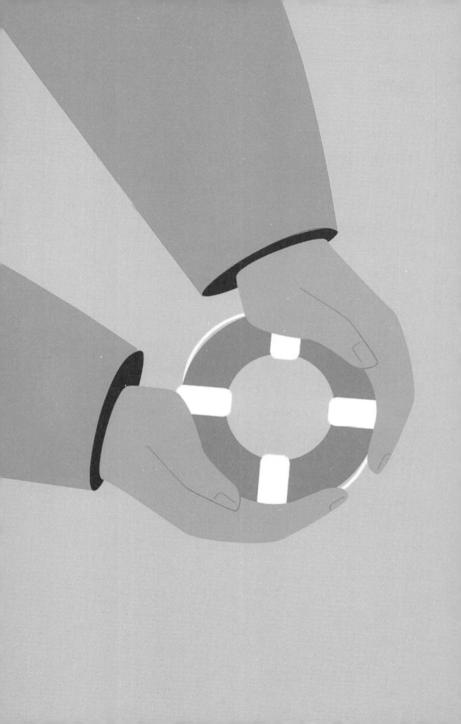

GOD'S 'BUT' HOLDS ALL AUTHORITY

**_But_ just say the word and my servant will be healed.
(Matthew 8:8)**

In Matthew 8, we read about a centurion who asks Jesus for help. His servant is severely ill and the centurion knows he needs a miracle. Both his humility and his faith in the situation are striking. He says to Jesus: 'I do not deserve to have you come under my roof. But just say the word and my servant will be healed' (Matt. 8:8).

The centurion had totally grasped the authority Jesus carries. Imagine ringing an ambulance if a loved one was seriously ill and saying, 'Don't bother coming to us, but just say one word and they'll be well.' I think we have an excellent health care system here in England, but it is not that good! Jesus, on the other hand, holds such power and authority that the centurion knew he really was that good. He absolutely believed that just one word from the mouth of Jesus – not even involving his physical presence – could bring complete healing.

How challenging for us in our own personal impossible situations.

Do we believe that Jesus could speak one word and everything would change for us? Do we believe that Jesus holds supreme power and authority, and because of that we are at rest because we know he is handling it for us?

I find it helpful in these testing times to remind myself of how amazing God is. To remember the incredible works and wonders he did in the Bible and also the things he's done and is doing in the lives of people I know. His authority is a hugely important dimension of his character that we must tap into. Having authority means 'having power, capability', 'being in control', 'having influence' and 'having the ability to "but in"'.

· Jesus can speak one word and somebody is completely healed. He has authority over sickness (Matt. 8:3).
· He spoke to a storm and it ceased. He has authority over the weather (Mark 4:35–41).
· He raised Lazarus from the dead. He has authority over death (John 11:38–44).
· He cast demons out of people and they were freed. He has authority over evil (Mark 5:1–20).
· He spoke and the world came into being. He calls out the stars by name. He has authority over creation (John 1:1–3).
· He died a horrific death to pay for our sin. He has authority over sin and death and desires for all of us to be free in him (Matt. 27:45–54).

In Matthew 28, Jesus states that 'all authority in heaven and on earth has been given to me'. He says this as part of the Great Commission, and he then tells the believers to go in his name, and to teach others how to be his disciples. He gives us *his* authority. That's an incredible privilege and responsibility – we carry the authority of Jesus. This doesn't mean that we strut around like Jim Carey's character Bruce Almighty, zapping everything that's near to us to the tune of 'I've Got the Power' (great scene to rewatch if you get a minute, though!). However, sometimes we skim over passages of the Bible so quickly and don't allow the truth of the words to sink in properly. Jesus tells us that we ourselves can walk in great levels of authority because he lives in us. The same power that raised Jesus from the dead lives in us (Rom. 8:11) – that is flippin' incredible! We must remember the authority he has, and that we also have as his followers, when faced with the challenges of life.

He rules, he reigns, he holds supreme authority. If he wants to 'but in' and cause something to happen, nothing can stop it. If we, like the centurion, can grasp the authority Jesus has, perhaps we will live at a different level of faith and see our circumstances turned around in Jesus' name.

> Then Jesus said to the centurion, 'Go! Let it be done just as you believed it would.' And his servant was healed at that moment.
>
> *Matt. 8:13*

One word from Jesus' mouth can change everything. Remind yourself today of the authority Jesus carries, and that he has commissioned you to now carry that same authority into your circumstances and your spheres of influence.

REFLECTION

The Bible says that without faith it
is impossible to please God
(Heb. 11:6). Why is putting our faith
in God's authority so important to him?
What does it show him?

Do you feel confident that Jesus has supreme authority?

Do you live in a way that acknowledges that you yourself
carry the authority of Jesus?

Are you in any way now tempted to strut down your
street singing, 'I've got the power'?

PRAYER

God, today I'm choosing to reflect on your supreme authority. When I look at the circumstances I'm facing, in
honesty, it often doesn't feel like you are in control. But
the truth is that you are, and I remind myself of your word
in Psalm 29:10 that says that you 'sit enthroned over the
flood'. I want to learn from the faith levels of the centurion in today's passage, who knew that just one word from
the mouth of Jesus was enough to change everything.
He must have really understood who you were – I want
to know you more, God, and to develop this level of faith
for myself. God, please help me to hold confidence and
assurance in your authority today. Remind me that you
have passed your authority on to me as your child – I want
to learn to walk in your authority. Amen.

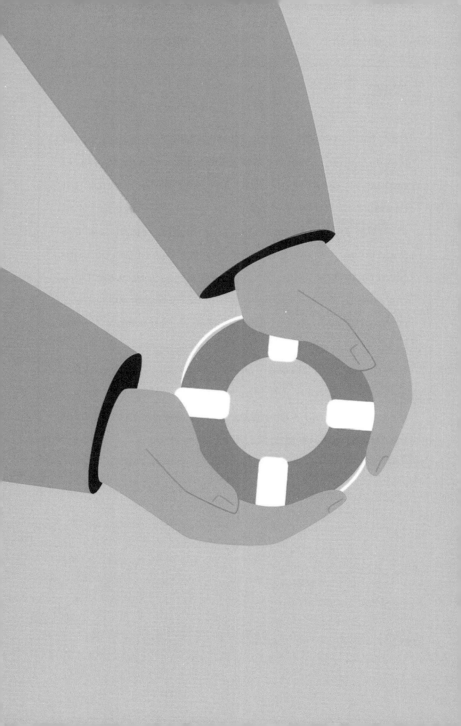

GOD'S 'BUT' KNOCKS THE ENEMY OUT OF THE WAY

But Caleb quieted the people before Moses, and said, 'Let us go up at once and occupy it, for we are well able to overcome it.' (Numbers 13:30, NRSV)

In Numbers 13, God tells Moses to send a group of people to Canaan to spy out the land. God said that he was giving this land of Canaan to the Israelites – it would be their promised land. All of the men who went to look were leaders of the Israelites. They had seen God do many miracles. They were directed by Moses to have a 'reet good nosey', as we'd say in Yorkshire, around Canaan and see how the land lay. How do people live? What are their towns like? Do they have big walls? Are there loads of them or just a few, and are the people strong or weak? What is the state of their soil and trees, and does the land produce good fruit? They spent forty days there and brought back some grapes, pomegranates and figs – even better quality than the super six selection we see in Aldi. Though I have to admit I'd want some decent chocolate truffles from a promised land, not just fruit and veg.

They then had to present a report to Moses, Aaron and the whole community of Israelites. They told them how the land was indeed flowing with milk and honey and they showed them the beautiful fruit selection. However, they had a big but – and it wasn't a positive one.

> But the people who live there are powerful, and the cities are fortified and very large. (Num. 13:28)

Their 'but' gets even bigger further on:

> 'We can't attack those people; they are stronger than we are.' And they spread among the Israelites a bad report . . . 'The land we explored devours those living in it. All the people we saw there are of great size . . . We seemed like grasshoppers in our own eyes, and we looked the same to them.'

Num. 13:31–3

As we have considered before, we don't need to deny problems and obstacles. We can acknowledge them and state they exist, and that's fine. If these men had reported what they had honestly seen, and followed it up with 'but they are no match for our God who has protected us and performed miracles for us before' then that's a different story. But that was not the case, they only focused on the natural negative circumstances.

God had said that Canaan would be their promised land. They had the promise of God over this situation. But they didn't believe they could overthrow the people living in Canaan as they were big and strong and looked like giants compared to them. I don't have an issue with humanly seeing the situation as they did, that was their natural assessment of it. However, they were not able to view it in light of God's promise that it would be their land. They didn't view it through God's eyes, or with God's ability to 'but in', in mind.

Then Caleb pipes up and changes the whole dynamic: '*[But]* Caleb silenced the people before Moses and said, "We should go up and take possession of the land, *for we can certainly do it*"' (Num. 13:30).

What incredible faith in the face of adversity. What an incredible overcoming spirit he had. He saw the same circumstances as the other leaders did, but he believed that God would help them conquer this land regardless of how tall and scary the people living there were. Caleb believed this because God had promised that Canaan was their promised land. Because God was able. Because God's 'but' can knock enemies clean out of your path.

In Numbers 14, the Israelites start complaining big time, wishing they had died in Egypt: 'Why is the LORD bringing us to this land only to let us fall by the sword?' (Num. 14:3).

They even consider ditching Moses, choosing a new leader and heading back to Egypt where they had faced horrendous lives of slavery. Joshua and Caleb, who had been to spy out Canaan, pipe up again. They highlight how amazing Canaan is, describing it as 'exceedingly good'. (I wonder if God could sue Mr Kipling for stealing that line!)

They go on to say:

> If the LORD is pleased with us, he will lead us into that land, a land flowing with milk and honey, and will give it to us. Only do not rebel against the LORD. And do not be afraid of the people of the land, because we will devour them. Their protection is gone, *but* the LORD is with us. Do not be afraid of them.
>
> *Num. 14:8–9*

I love how Joshua and Caleb say 'we will devour them', in comparison with all of the other negative Nigels who stated that the people of Canaan would devour the Israelites. Joshua and Caleb flip it on its head and say they will be doing the devouring.

The story has a bleak ending for the leaders who didn't believe God could help them overthrow Canaan. They all died of a plague. Joshua and Caleb were the only ones who survived.

Applying this to my own situation, I really want to have an overcoming attitude like Caleb and Joshua (and I really don't want to squiff it before entering the promised land like the negative Nigels). I want to develop a spirit that says, it may well look bleak, the enemy may look like giants and I may look like a grasshopper in comparison. But with God's help and because of what he has promised, I will face the enemy in God's power and I'm confident that God will win. We will conquer because almighty God is on our side. God's 'but' can knock any opposition out of my promised land.

Some situations we face in life are particularly big, scary and impossible-looking. I'm starting to understand that these are incredible opportunities to grow in faith in God, and I'm excited to see how he will work through my current challenge. I know I'm no match for a land full of giants on my own. But God can give me power to conquer and to overthrow the biggest of enemies that may be in front of me. And it's his big 'but' that clears my enemies out of the way so I can receive his promises.

REFLECTION

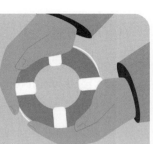

Be honest – are you more of a Joshua/Caleb or more of a negative Nigel at the moment? Are you more focused on the negative natural realities you see, or are you believing in God's promise to you and his ability to remove enemies from your promised land?

Reflect on the faith-building attitude Joshua and Caleb had and think about how you can personally follow their example – and give Neggy Nige the heave-ho.

Be honest – would you want a cucumber or a salted caramel truffle from a promised land? I might get a bit distracted by devouring said truffles rather than devouring enemies though, if I'm being honest.

PRAYER

God, I really want to develop this overcoming attitude that Caleb and Joshua had. They saw the natural realities but they kept your promise to them at the front of their hearts and minds. Because of their deep trust in you, they weren't phased by the giants, they knew that because you were on their side they could 'certainly' take possession of the promised land. I acknowledge my leaning towards being a negative Nigel and I recognise how easily I can become overwhelmed by the difficulties within my situation. Today I focus on your ability to knock any enemies out of the way of the promises you have given to me. Amen.

GOD'S 'BUT' CAN TURN AROUND

You intended to harm me, *but* God intended it for good to accomplish what is now being done, the saving of many lives. (Genesis 50:20)

My husband and I have just finished watching *When They See Us* on Netflix – I have to admit it wrecked me emotionally! It's an incredibly moving story of five young black men who are wrongfully accused of assault, rape and attempted murder. The police involved at a high level were corrupt and coerced them into making statements admitting they did it, but none of them were guilty at all. Thankfully the person who committed the crime confessed, albeit years later, and they were subsequently released. They all spent between six and fourteen years wrongfully imprisoned.

We watched Oprah interview them and I cried as I saw the pain that two of them particularly still so deeply carry. This level of horrendous injustice is truly difficult to watch. I admire these men so much for rebuilding their lives as best as they can following their release. I pray they will all find true healing and peace despite the horrific years of their lives spent in prison, the mistreatment and abuse they were subject to and the wrongful accusations made against them. Harrowing stuff.

It reminded me of a character in the Bible who faced a similar trial. It's the man with the jazzy dressing-gown, otherwise known as Joseph. Joseph was a cocky little rascal in his early life. He had dreams of his brothers bowing down to him. These were God-inspired dreams, but he didn't have the common sense to keep his trap shut about them. His brothers hated him because of this, and also because they could see he was daddy's favourite, decked out in his bespoke jazzy dressing-gown.

Joseph's brothers threw him in a pit and left him for dead. But then some Egyptians passed by and instead he was sold into slavery. His brothers told his dad he had been killed by wild animals. Joseph worked hard and impressed his boss, Potiphar, and earned himself a good job in his household. Potiphar's wife took a fancy to Joseph and tried to get him in the sack. But Joseph kept refusing, which made her so mad that she accused him of attempting to assault her.

Joseph then went to prison. God's favour was on him in prison and the guard put him in charge of the other prisoners. He was able to interpret the dreams of two men in prison with him and both interpretations were true and came to pass. But this was then forgotten. He spent a further two years in prison.

Two flippin' years.

That's a long time to be forgotten.

Yet he didn't become bitter. (I would've backslidden within about twenty minutes.)

Eventually, when Pharoah needed a dream interpreter, Joseph was remembered and he told Pharaoh what his dream meant.

He was then put in a hugely powerful position, similar to the role of a prime minister. During a severe famine, his brothers had to come to him and ask for food.

He eventually reveals his identity to them. He doesn't hate them or make them pay for what they did to him. (I want to punch my husband in the face just for not making the bed, so this level of grace really does blow my mind!) Joseph is loving and gracious, and recognises that while they may have intended harm to come to him, God's goodness turned the situation around. This meant many lives were saved through what Joseph did – and through his gracious and forgiving attitude.

The many challenges he faced in his life turned that cocky little rascal into a godly, powerful, yet humble prime minister.

God doesn't always 'but in' and prevent rubbish circumstances in our lives. It's difficult for us to understand this, as we know he holds the power to do so. We wonder how a kind, good and all-powerful God could allow us to go through times of significant pain, trials and even injustice. This is where God's turnaround 'but' comes into its own.

Reflecting on my situation, in honesty, I would much prefer for it to all have gone smoothly and to be living out my dream by now. But. If this had been the case, I would not be digging deep in my faith as I am right now, standing on his promises over my life more than ever, declaring his truth over my impossible situation, believing and trusting in him at a level I never have done before. In past trials I have not always responded as I have this time. But this time, I'm looking at the Bible through fresh eyes. Not just seeing the stories as Sunday-school stories, but reminding myself that these things really happened. Activating faith, hope, confidence and belief that

God not only can, but that he will turn this situation around. This time I'm not becoming bitter and stressed, but I am expecting God to move. There's a degree to which I'm actually glad to have this opportunity to stand in faith and see God 'but in' and make a way. It will take a miracle and I'm confident this will happen.

All kinds of people and circumstances in our lives can intend to harm us with their actions, words and motives. We may well suffer as a consequence of this and spend more time than we would like learning some hard lessons, even though we haven't necessarily done anything wrong. At these times we can choose to wait, like Joseph did, in anticipation of God's turnaround 'but'.

I love how Joseph's heart remains soft and forgiving towards his brothers. He had every right to punish them, make them squirm and ensure they had no essential supplies (literally what I think is an appropriate punishment for my husband's unmade bed). He really could've made them pay. But his attitude is incredible. He somehow is able to see God at work within the dire circumstances his brothers forced him into. He fully acknowledges God's turnaround 'but'. They intended to harm him, but God intended it for good – and as a result many lives were saved. Joseph was given insight by God into there being seven prosperous years and then seven years of famine, so Joseph was able to prepare well and ensure there was enough supply for all.

God's 'but in' turned everything around for Joseph, and in turn saved many people's lives. There are many others who will potentially be influenced by you trusting in God in your situation and keeping a good attitude. Let's do our best to believe with 'jazzy robe Joe' that God will 'but in' and provide a turnaround for us too.

Today I want to challenge us about the way we are walking through this difficult time. We have the power to do so like Joseph did, in love, without bitterness and having a positive impact on others (admittedly easier said than done). Our words and behaviour through our challenging circumstances have great potential to inspire faith and hope in others around us.

REFLECTION

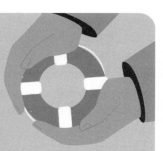

During testing times it's very easy to become bitter, especially if we feel unfairly treated. Do you feel any bitterness? Is that directed towards God or towards others?

Reflect on the life of Joseph and the injustice he experienced. He was sold into slavery by his brothers who then told his dad he was dead; he was imprisoned for two years, forgotten about by people who promised to remember and rescue him, and falsely accused of assault. That's a lot. How do you think he came through all of that with such a good attitude?

How can you apply what you've learnt from Joseph and the way he navigated the unfairness of his situation to what you are currently experiencing?

If you have any tips on how to get a spouse to make the bed, please do reach out and educate me, thank you.

PRAYER

God, the story of Joseph is an amazing example of your ability to turn around dire and unjust situations for good. Joseph experienced betrayal, false allegations, being forgotten, and a long period of waiting in prison for a crime he hadn't committed. Somehow, despite all of this he was able to transform from a cocky little rascal into a godly prime minister. Please help me to remember your ability to turn my situation around in your timing, and to embrace the opportunities for growth as I wait for you to do this. Help me to keep a soft and gracious heart towards those around me as Joseph did. I don't want to become impatient and bitter; I want to grow in endurance and wisdom like Joseph. Amen.

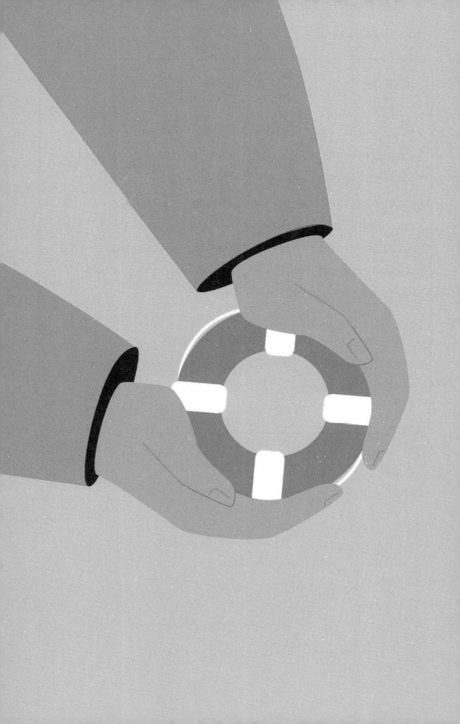

GOD'S 'BUT' CAN MOVE MOUNTAINS

But also you can say to this mountain, 'Go, throw yourself into the sea' and it will be done. (Matthew 21:21)

This verse is particularly apt for me right now in the middle of our impossible situation. I have a dream to do something which I believe is a huge part of God's calling on my life. God has confirmed he is in it, he has spoken clearly through his word. But the reality presented to me is that the 'big cheese' who makes the final decision at our fostering agency is 'very unlikely' to let us proceed with this dream.

Last night we had some encouraging news that a panel has met to further discuss our case and unanimously agreed we should be able to proceed. This was the best possible outcome we could've hoped for at this point and it was lovely to have that affirmation.

But.

There's still that big cheese who is not very keen on the idea of us proceeding. What the big cheese says goes ultimately, despite the extremely supportive feedback from the group who met last night. It's at times like this that I'm extremely glad that I have a personal relationship with the biggest of cheeses whose name is Jesus! (Love a bit of Christian rhyme!) But seriously, I'm taking such comfort and confidence knowing God has all of this in hand. He has gone before us, he has made a way for us – I'm really believing it's a done deal and that soon he will divinely 'but in' on our behalf.

I admit that when I reflect back to the conversation where we were encouraged to withdraw because we were 'highly unlikely' to be successful, I start to wobble. When I look through my natural eyes, the mountain appears to be huge and firmly planted right in my way. So today particularly I have been speaking out this verse about moving mountains and looking at my situation with eyes of faith. Speaking to mountains is not an airy-fairy tree-huggers type of concept for people who like talking to the forest and rolling around in leaves, etc. (whatever floats your boat). It's a real decla-ration of faith to speak to the mountains/obstacles in our way and believe for God to do something impossible.

A mountain is a huge, heavy, immovable object that is slap bang in between us and our dream or promise. There's even a big cheese on top of my mountain. But thankfully there's an even bigger cheese who can in a second clear the path. Interestingly though, God tells *us* to do the work of moving the mountain, which involves great levels of faith. We must resist doubt and be as faith-filled as we can, and partner with him in shifting 'Ben Nevis o'clock'. He is able, but we must join with him and activate our faith, using our own mouths to speak to the mountains in front of us.

I'm currently reading the gospels and it's clear how much Jesus responded to people's faith. He was openly impressed by the faith some people had. We've already looked at the centurion who knew Jesus just needed to speak a word and his servant would be healed. There's the woman with the issue of blood who knew if she touched even the edge of his cloak she would be healed. There are also the four blokes who desperately wanted Jesus to heal their friend and lowered him through the roof to make it happen. These levels of faith really impressed Jesus, because these people had mountain-moving faith.

- Then Jesus said to the centurion, 'Go! Let it be done just as you believed it would.' And his servant was healed at that moment. (Matt. 8:13)
- He said to her, 'Daughter, your faith has healed you. Go in peace and be freed from your suffering.' (Mark 5:34)
- When Jesus saw their faith, he said to the paralysed man, 'Son, your sins are forgiven.' (Mark 2:5)

One of my favourite people in the Bible is a woman whose name we don't know, but she had such a feisty level of faith that it greatly impressed Jesus. I think we need to follow this sassy sister's lead and persist in faith for our breakthrough because we recognise that Jesus truly can 'but in' and transform our impossible situation.

The mountain in front of this woman was a big one – her daughter was possessed by a demon. She was a mamma who was desperate for her daughter to be healed. She was a Canaanite woman – a Gentile, which meant she was an enemy of the Jews. The dialogue between her and Jesus is quite an uncomfortable read and I've struggled with this passage for a long time, because of the way Jesus speaks to her. It's almost like Jesus himself is acting as a mountain blocking her miracle.

She comes to him and begs him to heal her daughter and he promptly tells her that his mission is to save the Jews, as at this point in the Bible that was his primary focus. But she won't let it drop – she wants to see her daughter healed and she recognised that Jesus had the power to 'but in' and cast out the demon from her daughter.

Jesus says to her, 'It's not right to take the children's bread and toss it to the dogs' (Matt. 15:26) – meaning that he has come for the Jews and not the Gentiles. Surely Jesus could have phrased his let-down in a nicer way? Undeterred by his apparently offensive refusal to help, she challenges Jesus, saying, 'Yes it is, Lord . . . Even the dogs eat the crumbs that fall from their master's table' (15:27). It's an unusual text, as Jesus so often comes across as compassionate and loving and it can appear here that he's harsh and blatantly rude. Her quick-witted, bold, faith-fuelled comeback however really grabs Jesus' attention. He is impressed by this sassy lassie, so much that he says, 'Woman, you have great faith! Your request is granted.' Her daughter experienced healing the moment he said those words.

I have grown to love this story that I've wrestled to understand over the years, as this bold woman challenges Jesus and he takes note and acts because of her faith. Wow! In a patriarchal culture where women were second class, this Gentile woman who had so much stacked against her refuses to be held back by cultural norms and steps forward in boldness and mountain-moving faith. She uses her voice to speak to the mountain in front of her. She effectively tells Jesus he is wrong, and he changes his mind and grants her request. Incredible.

Feisty, mountain-moving faith is something we need to do our best to take hold of.

Feisty faith gets the attention of Jesus. God responds to feisty faith. Mountains are no problem to him, so let's place our faith in his ability to 'but in' and let's speak his truth to the mountains in front of us.

> Now faith is confidence in what we hope for and assurance about what
> we do not see.
>
> *Heb. 11:1*

Dear Big Cheese,

Fair enough for you to not Brie hasty and consider our case Caer-
philly. However, now just halloumi to proceed with this dream.
Cheddar move on, I don't give Edam for waiting any longer.

Kind regards,

Kate (slightly crackers and getting in a pickle with all this waiting)

REFLECTION

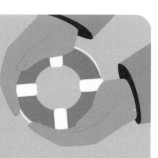

Where would you say your faith
levels are at currently? Are you more
focused on the mountain or are you
able to focus on God who can move
the mountain?

Are you confident of what you are hoping for and certain
of what you do not yet see? What can you practically do
to increase your faith for God to 'but in' today?

How feisty is your faith? How do you feel about the Canaanite woman's feisty response to Jesus? How can you
apply this to your own impossible situation?

How do you feel about it being your job to speak to the
mountains in your way? Do you feel confident to tell Ben
Nevis to 'do one'? If not, how can you develop your faith
levels?

PRAYER

God, I thank you for involving us in your purposes. You don't just wave a magic wand and remove an obstacle, you invite us to partner with you and to use our own mouths to speak to any mountains that are in between us and the things you have promised us. Your word empowers and equips us with all we need to stand firm in the face of adversity. I really desire to grow in my belief in your power, and in the way that your power can work through me as I open my mouth and speak your truths over my situation. Help me to be bold in my confession – give me courage and help me cultivate a feisty faith similar to the Canaanite woman, so I can face Ben Nevis o'clock with your strength and wisdom. Amen.

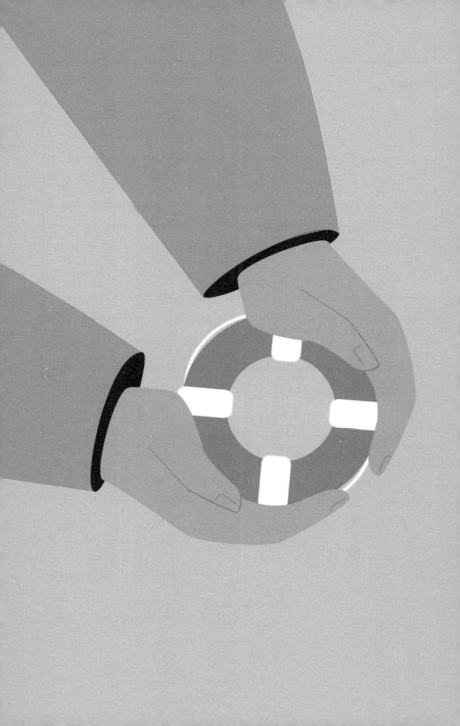

YOU CAN'T ALWAYS SEE GOD'S 'BUT'

So we fix our eyes not on what is seen, *but* on what is unseen, since what is seen is temporary, *but* what is unseen is eternal. (2 Corinthians 4:18)

As I sat down to write today, a song called 'It is Well' came on. The lyrics encourage us to believe and have faith even when our eyes see no evidence of God being at work. It felt really timely because of the line of thought I had for today's devotion. So let's have a good look at the theme of God's unseen 'but'. Just because it's unseen certainly does not mean it is not there, or it is not hard at work behind the scenes.

The verse from 2 Corinthians 4:18 is such an important one for us to remember. If you are anything like me, the temptation to be swamped, discouraged and defeated by the 'seen' is strong. Throughout this challenge I'm facing I have been encouraged as I consider the supernatural and eternal, and to choose to focus on those incredible, yet often unseen truths, rather than the temporary 'seen' facts in front of me.

I often forget that there is a whole unseen spiritual world out there, including both good and evil. Ephesians 6:12 says: 'For our struggle is not against flesh and blood, but against the rulers, against the authorities, against the powers of this dark world and against the spiritual forces of evil in the heavenly realms.' This seems very intense, but as unseen as it may appear to us, this spiritual realm is very real. As Christians we know that God ultimately holds all power and authority and so we do not need to fear this. We do however need to recognise and understand the very real battle we face. Ephesians 6 goes on to describe how putting on the armour of God enables us to stand against these dark spiritual powers effectively. We've got all the right gear so there's no need to fear! (You are welcome – feel free to get that printed on a T-shirt!)

I think I have lived a large amount of my life being fairly ignorant about these things. There is certainly a balance to be found – I've heard it said that some Christians 'see a demon under every cornflake'! We don't need to be preoccupied with dark forces, and go looking for trouble, so to speak. But we need to be aware that we have an enemy who is very real and who wants to steal, kill and destroy. Fortunately, we are on the winning team with Jesus who counters that with bringing us life in all its fullness. John 10:10 says, 'The thief comes only to steal, kill and destroy; I have come that they may have life, and have it to the full.'

How we talk about these unseen powers is important too. At our wedding someone leading at the front said, 'The enemy would love to destroy this marriage.' We believe this is true and we understand that he was referring to the devil wanting to oppose our marriage and cause it to fail. However, a member of the congregation who was not well acquainted with church jargon quietly said, 'Does he mean the Russians?'!

I remember reading a book before we adopted our little girl and the writer stated that he felt adoption was 'spiritual warfare'.

He said that the devil hates adoption and he explained the high price Jesus had to pay for our adoption. I felt like he needed to chill out a bit, to be honest, when I read it at the time. Now, however, being on the other side of an adoption and the intense emotional distress we experienced, I'm a lot more inclined to agree with him. The devil hates the fact that children who have been abused, neglected or abandoned find safe and loving homes where they can find healing, acceptance and belonging. No wonder there's a backlash of opposition often seen when we attempt to do things to love and bless others.

I believe there are dark forces at work aiming to do their best to prevent some of our dreams being fulfilled because there is a lot of good riding on them. When we have a dream from God and we know our motives are right and it will bless others, we can expect significant opposition. But we must remember that although these spiritual forces can cause problems, spanners in the works and discouragement, God has the final say.

I love this verse from Job 42:2: 'I know that you can do all things; no purpose of yours can be thwarted.' (If you are a fan of the British show, *Miranda*, I'm sure you'll agree that 'thwarted' is definitely a word that she would say, then look at the camera, repeat and giggle!) Isaiah 43:13 records God saying: 'When I act, who can reverse it?' These are the truths we need to be clinging onto during times of intense opposition.

The difficulties we face do not take God by surprise. He's not reclining on a cloud one minute and throwing his heavenly harp to one side in a panic the next because there's been a plot twist. He knows the end from the beginning. Not only is he all-knowing, but he is constantly working things out for our good. This can often be the unseen part from our perspective. God is at work on our behalf. A friend recently encouraged us with a Scripture from Exodus 14:14 (AMP): 'The LORD will fight for you while you [only need to] keep silent and remain calm.' God fights our battles. God manoeuvres situations and circumstances on our behalf. God can 'but in' and change hearts and minds. Often, this work he is doing is completely unseen by us.

The song 'Way Maker' has really connected with the hearts of many people in the last few years. It declares that God is always at work, even when we can't see it or feel it. This is such truth – we often cannot see or feel what God is up to. It may even appear that he's doing nothing at all. But he cares, he fights, he manoeuvres, he plans things for our good and for his glory – despite a lot of this being unseen by ourselves.

I have said to God many times over this last month, 'God, I can't see how you are going to remove this mountain, but that's not my job. My job is to cling to the promises you've spoken to us and to trust you and confess your truth over it.' I have recently prayed quite differently from how I have prayed before. I heard a preacher say that when you pray you should bring God's promises to him. So I haven't been saying, 'God, please can you do A, B and C? Thank you and kind regards'! I've brought the words and promises he's spoken to us back to him and in doing so my faith and confidence are high. I haven't begged God to do the thing I would do to fix this situation if I was him. I've stepped back and said, 'OK, God, you have spoken and said you will bless this, so you do it your way and I'll stand back and let you crack on.' (I hope God is OK with me giving him my permission to crack on!)

Be assured today that God's 'but' is at work even when it's unseen.

REFLECTION

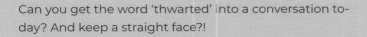

Can you currently see what
God is up to in your situation?

Can you reflect on any past situations
where God was at work but you
couldn't see it at the time?

Can you get the word 'thwarted' into a conversation today? And keep a straight face?!

If you have time, I'd really encourage you to listen to
Priscilla Shirer, 'When it Feels Like God is Doing Nothing' –
type it into YouTube and her sermon on this topic will
come up. It's good stuff.

PRAYER

God, sometimes it feels like you are nowhere to be seen. I pray, and I don't feel you are listening. I seek you and I want to know your heart but I can't hear or sense anything. I pray that during these dark and confusing times, I will hold on to what I know to be true. You are good, you love me, you can be trusted. You are always at work even when it seems that the opposite is true. You are working behind the scenes in ways I cannot perceive. You want the best for me and I resolve today to submit to your plans and your timetable. Amen.

DAY 14

GOD REFINES US SO THAT WE REFLECT HIS 'BUT'

**_But_ he knows the way that I take; when he has tested me,
I will come forth as gold. (Job 23:10)**

My husband recently filmed a short talk to encourage his work colleagues. He focused on how God works to refine us. Often in challenging times, we feel like we are under intense heat and pressure. Even though this may not feel pleasant, there is a lot of good that can come from it. When a metal worker heats a substance, the impurities all come to the surface. They then skim the impurities off. This process is repeated until all impurities are gone and the metal worker can see their own reflection clearly in the metal. This is a powerful picture of what God does in us during times of intense trial. We often hear this referred to as a process called 'refining'.

Refining means 'to bring something to a fine or pure state', 'to free from impurities'. God desires us to look more like him. We want to reflect our Heavenly Father, and the refining process gives great opportunity for this. When we come against problems, stress and difficult circumstances, we are often faced with the impurities within us. For example, in my own situation, I have realised how I have a tendency towards wanting to be in control. I'm prone to being anxious about what I see happening around me, rather than looking at a situation through a lens of faith, and I tend to be pessimistic rather than optimistic.

I have had to seriously address each of these impurities. I've had to realise that the situation is totally out of my control, but rejoice that it is completely under God's control. I've realised that it does not matter what the biggest of all human cheeses tells me – if I have faith in God's promises, he will see that they come to pass. It's his voice I must listen to and trust despite what all other voices may say. I've had to dig deep to remain in a place of faith and confidence that God will do a miracle, to daily declare his word and not wobble in unbelief and defeat. I've had to determine to take joy in each day despite the waiting and uncertainty which has dragged on for months.

I have been refined in a way I never have before. But my level of faith has increased. I have clung to his word at a different level than I have before. I'm genuinely expecting him to do a miracle.

I would never have chosen this trial, but I have to admit it has served as a great tool for many impurities to come to the surface. Next time I go through this process there will likely be a whole host of other impurities to be skimmed off. But for now, I'm thankful that I've learnt a lot and grown a lot even though in honesty it's also been a right pain in my butt!

I don't believe God causes awful things to happen to us so we can be refined. We've explored previously the spiritual realm and the forces of evil that seek to bring destruction. But I believe that within the difficult times, God stands at our side and cheers us on. He walks with us through the struggles of refining, and gives us strength, endurance, hope and encouragement.

These verses from 1 Peter 1:6–7 help us understand God's refining:

> In all this you greatly rejoice, though now for a little while you may have had to suffer grief in all kinds of trials. These have come so that the proven genuineness of your faith – of greater worth than gold, which perishes even though refined by fire – may result in praise, glory and honour when Jesus Christ is revealed.

In refining, we get to prove how genuine our faith is. And genuine faith is more valuable to God than gold.

It's very easy to trot out biblical statements about mountains and mustard seeds when there's nothing at stake. But when faced with human impossibilities, it's then we have an opportunity to prove if we have true faith in God. God is so concerned with our faith and character being genuine. This brings real glory to him – as those around us see people at peace and in confidence amid extremely difficult circumstances. We can only do this because of knowing God in a personal way; being assured that he is who he says he is.

We don't need to ever fake faith. I love the man in the Gospel of Mark 9:24 who says to Jesus, 'I do believe, help me overcome my unbelief.' This man was being refined. His faith levels were being tested. He had faith, but there was a deeper genuineness of faith for him to find.

Let's be honest with God about where we are at. Let's ask him to raise our levels of faith. And let's ask him to scoop off those impurities so we can reflect him and his 'but' as much as we possibly can.

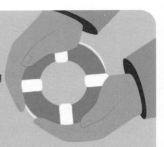

REFLECTION

What impurities is this trial bringing
up to be skimmed off in your life?

Have any of these impurities taken
you by surprise?

Do you feel you are being refined and that your faith is
growing as a result?

What do you feel your life is reflecting to those around
you?

PRAYER

God, refining is a painful process. So many impurities are evident in my life. I want to reflect you well, so I embrace this process of facing up to my flaws and I take this opportunity to become more like you. I want to change, to deepen my faith in you. I want others to see a reflection of your character through the way I deal with this difficulty. I need so much help with this. Please give me grace, help me to be kind to myself as I bring my weaknesses and shortcomings to you. Thank you that you love me warts and all, and you are cheering me on as I walk through this process of refining. Amen.

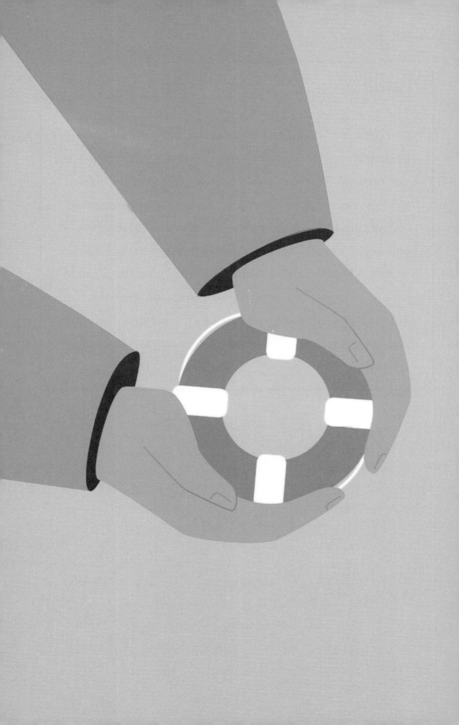

GOD'S 'BUT' PROPS US UP

So Joshua fought the Amalekites as Moses had ordered, and Moses, Aaron and Hur went to the top of the hill. As long as Moses held up his hands, the Israelites were winning, *but* whenever he lowered his hands, the Amalekites were winning. When Moses' hands grew tired, they took a stone and put it under him and he sat on it. Aaron and Hur held his hands up – one on one side, one on the other – so that his hands remained steady till sunset. So Joshua overcame the Amalekite army with the sword. (Exodus 17:10–13)

This passage of Scripture is often used to highlight the importance of friendship, community and bearing one another's burdens. All of us get tired and weary in our various life battles. We all need the support of others and at times to experience the strength that comes when we allow others to take some of the strain for us. We also need to in turn take the strain for others.

I find this an encouraging story as it demonstrates that we cannot be self-reliant and do it all on our own. We often like to pretend we can and that we are strong and don't really need others. But I really believe that every person on this planet is struggling with a whole host of different issues, no one is the finished article who is perfect and self-sufficient. Not even burning-bush-talking, water-from-a-rock, sea-parting Moses! If Moses needed friends to lend a hand – then we, without exception, also do.

Moses had done amazing things for God and had seen God do amazing things. He could have felt like he had 'made it' in many respects, and rejected the help from Aaron and Hur in holding up his hands. But he didn't, he accepted this much-needed help. It's at this point my husband would likely say: 'It takes teamwork to make the dream work' and I would want to roll my eyes and sarcastically suggest he gets the dishes done pronto in that case! But we really do need each other, and the battle was indeed won by teamwork. Most battles involve teamwork at some level.

God designed us to be a community, a body of people, looking out for each other, celebrating with each other and helping each other. We need to both give and receive in all of these areas to really thrive in life. Galatians 6:2 says: 'Carry each other's burdens, and in this way you will fulfil the law of Christ.' This is a bold command, not a fluffy 'be nice to each other' type of sentiment – it's a call for us to carry the weight of each other's burdens. In doing so we fulfil Jesus' commands.

During my current challenge, I am so thankful for the people God has put around me who are holding my hands up, so to speak. Friends and family who have prayed, fasted, prophesied, sent flowers, texted encouraging messages and Scriptures, and really believed along with us that God is going to 'but in' and transform this situation. I have drawn a lot of strength from this and very much appreciate their love and support. It's hard sometimes to admit you are struggling, feeling weak and that you need help. But honesty and vulnerability bring a real depth to relationships. I've had to admit to some close people that this has been one of the most difficult years of my life. But in doing so, people I trust have been a huge source of strength and encouragement. I would not be thriving in this process as I am if it wasn't for them.

Overall, I've been really positive during this challenge and remained in faith for most of it. Yesterday was a tough day, though. It could be that it was just a rough day, or that I'm just fed up with living in this limbo. We are also in the middle of a coronavirus pandemic, with the uncertainty involved with that and not knowing when we can see friends and family again. But whatever the reasons, yesterday was a 'cheesed off' day. I messaged my mum and she reminded me of some of God's promises over this situation. This didn't resolve our circumstances, but it did give me strength to get through the day, and reminded me that I'm not going through this alone. My arms were lifted and supported as the battle continues.

Sometimes it can be tempting to sit in our little pity party, or not to reach out for help as we don't want to be a burden. But I know that if one of my friends was feeling rubbish, I'd really want to be there for them. We must get over our excuses for not asking for help and just chuffin' well do it.

From the story of the battle we opened with, it's really important to remember that this battle would not have been won if it were not for Aaron and Hur. The role they played in holding up Moses' hands was absolutely vital. When Moses' hands dropped, the Amalekites started to win. Joshua was on the front line fighting the battle. Moses was watching on a hill and interceding for the people. Aaron and Hur's role in holding up his arms should not be downplayed. We all need our people – our 'his and Hur's' if you will (!) to be at our side holding up our arms in battle.

So today let's reflect on those people God has graciously given to us. Let's thank him for them, and let's make sure we are being honest with them about where we are at and how they can support us. Let's also consider whose arms we are holding up. Is there a friend who may need us today? That might look like a phone call, an encouraging text, half an hour praying with or for them, a bunch of flowers, a coffee date. Let's hold up each other's arms and, in doing so, see many victories in our battles.

REFLECTION

Who are you allowing to hold
up your arms in this challenging
situation you are facing?

Is there anyone else you need to
enlist support from?

Are you supporting anyone else with their challenge?

How can you practically hold someone's arms up today?

PRAYER

God, I thank you for this biblical example of how much we need each other. None of us is self-sufficient, we all need people around us to 'hold up our arms' when things get tough. This biblical battle was won because these people worked together – I acknowledge the indispensable role Aaron and Hur played in holding up Moses' arms. I acknowledge that I too need people to hold up my arms through my own personal battle. Help me to be brave enough to ask for help and give me wisdom to identify the right people to ask help and advice from. Help me also to look for others who need their arms holding up, to stand with other brothers and sisters who are experiencing different battles from mine. Thank you for your church – your body. Help us to be united and supportive of one another, carrying each other's burdens as you have commanded. Amen.

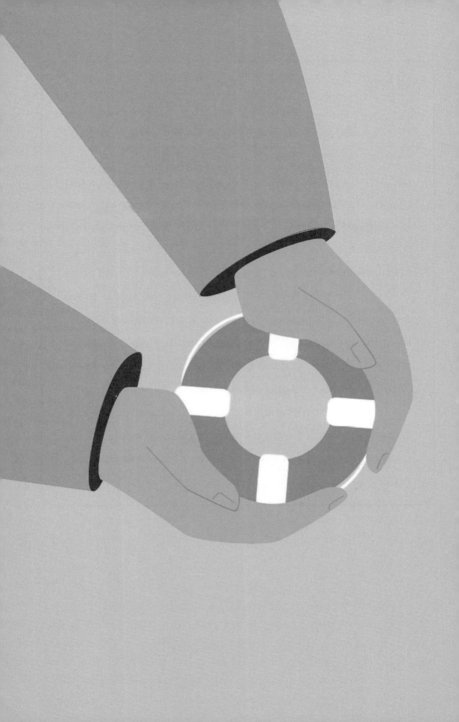

GOD'S 'BUT' PERFORMS MIRACLES

'*But* I know that even now God will give you whatever you ask.' Jesus said to her, 'Your brother will rise again.'
(John 11:22–3)

I'm currently reading through the gospels and what really strikes me is the faith of the women who followed Jesus. I've heard it said that Jesus' female followers were 'the last at the cross and the first at the tomb'. I also love how Jesus engages with women and shares some of his most intimate moments with them. He included women in his circle of friendship even though this would have been frowned upon within their culture. This meant that women such as Martha from today's passage were able to have a deeply personal relationship with him and therefore had the opportunity to hold a great level of faith in him.

'But I know that even now God will give you whatever you ask' are Martha's words. She was the sister of Lazarus and a close friend of Jesus. She is grieving as her brother has died and she knows if Jesus had been present, he could've prevented it. That shows great faith in itself, to believe Jesus had the power to heal her extremely ill brother. But he isn't ill now, he's brown bread – dead – toast. The end of his life – game over. Future family plans ruined, no hope, nothing more we can do. Or is there? Martha dared to believe that Jesus had the power to do anything, even to raise the dead. Martha knew that with Jesus, death was not the end, it did not have the final word. Incredible levels of faith!

'But . . . even now.' Even when things look, feel and appear dead, Martha trusted that Jesus could bring hope, life and miraculous intervention. She really knew Jesus – she trusted him so much and had great faith in him and the power he held. Many people did not even recognise Jesus as the Messiah as he wasn't an Incredible Hulk enemy-bashing warrior-type. But Martha knew who he was, because she had an intimate relationship with him – she truly knew him. Her levels of faith inspire me so much in my own situation. Humanly speaking we have been told the dream is as good as dead, it's highly unlikely to happen. So either I focus on the negative things that professionals involved have said to us, or I focus on what God has spoken over our situation and I declare with Martha that even though the dream looks dead, we can have an 'even now' miraculous moment.

I love plaques with funny or cute things written on – I've got them all over my house! My friend asked if I wanted one of hers that said: 'Expect a miracle' on it. I have to admit that for ages I've battled whether to even have this up. It's hard. As I've said before I'm not a prosperity gospel fan at all. I worried that it might look like that's what I'm advocating in having that plaque in my home. The cheesy kind of hyper-positive thinking that God is always ready round every corner to shower you with money and cars and whatever else you might fancy (no idea why Daniel Craig just popped into my head!). When people are facing really tough times and feeling the opposite of blessed and prospering, this thinking can be a right slap in the face and make them feel like they are failing.

We all face suffering and difficulties, we don't skip from one happy and prosperous event to another. Sometimes life is ruddy hard – I've never seen a plaque with that written on! However, I have had second thoughts about my 'expect a miracle' plaque. I think with the right motivation and intent, it's absolutely right to expect God to do a miracle. When the outcome is for our good and his glory, why not look for a miracle? Our God is a wonder-working God! He turned water to wine, healed all kinds of diseases, raised the dead – there is nothing he can't do! I think 'expect a miracle' was Martha's attitude, because she really knew Jesus and understood his divine authority and his ability to 'but in' and drastically change impossible situations.

I'm holding onto examples of great faith like Martha's, and joining with her in believing that 'even now', God can turn this dead situation around. He can bring new life where there is death and darkness and despair. If God has spoken to you, but all seems dead and hopeless – expect a miracle. This is not a Disney-style dreamy notion. If your faith and expectation are in Jesus and what he said he will do for you then stand strong in that. He is the God who raised Lazarus from the dead.

If you are in an 'even now' situation, expect a miracle.

REFLECTION

How does the phrase 'expect a
miracle' make you feel?

What do you think about Martha's levels
of faith? How did her close relationship
with Jesus impact on her levels of faith and expectation?

Can you pray a 'but even now' prayer over your impossible
situation?

PRAYER

God, I'm so inspired by Martha's belief in your ability to do the impossible. I recognise that her belief came out of an intimate relationship with you. She spent quality time in your presence and this shows in her level of faith in you. Help me to prioritise time with you, getting to know you more so I can have an increased level of confidence in your power as Martha did. I want to believe that 'even now', when hopes and dreams are as good as dead, you can miraculously intervene in my situation. Today I expect a miracle, and I believe for you to breathe your life into the situations I'm facing that seem dark, dead and hopeless. Amen.

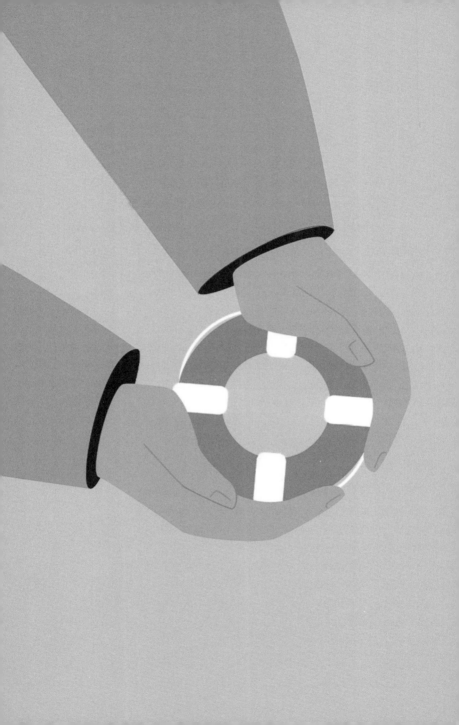

GOD'S 'BUT' DOES NOT SHRINK BACK

For the Spirit God gave us does not make us timid, *but* gives us power, love and self-discipline. (2 Timothy 1:7)

'Timid' is defined as showing a lack of courage or confidence, and being easily frightened. It's very easy to shrink back in timidity, fear and defeat when we are up against some impossible situations. But the Spirit of God gives us the opposite of timidity. With God's Spirit we can go forward in power, love and self-discipline. I love the incredible combination of these three qualities – let's look at all three and consider their importance.

Power

It goes against how we most likely feel in our tough situations. I feel pretty powerless, in honesty, as there's nothing I can do to influence or change our situation for good. This is an exciting position to be in, though, because it means I have to fully rely on God's power to 'but in' and change it. Just because I don't hold any power over the situation, does not mean I cannot feel powerful. I need to align myself with God's word, his promises and his power. In doing so my thinking, behaviour and confession can become powerful, not timid. Power, like confidence and peace, is not always loud and proud. Power can be seen in a steadfast, calm and confident spirit. You demonstrate power when you have control over your mind and emotions and you don't let the situation get you down when it could quite easily take you out.

Power is defined as the ability to direct or change the behaviour of others, or the course of events. I certainly cannot do any of this in our challenge. But I can align my mind and emotions with the fact that my God certainly can direct and change the course of events. All power belongs to him. His Spirit lives in me and if he says his Spirit gives us power then I can walk in that power.

Love

I wondered why love was included in this Scripture. What's love got to do, got to do with it? Having reflected on this I realised that it's a real challenge to have a spirit of love, particularly when you are in a time of strong adversity. When we think about the famous 'luuurve' Scriptures from 1 Corinthians 13, we see how multifaceted love is:

> Love is patient, love is kind. It does not envy, it does not boast, it is not proud. It does not dishonour others, it is not self-seeking, it is not easily angered, it keeps no record of wrongs. Love does not delight in evil but rejoices with the truth. It always protects, always trusts, always hopes, always perseveres.
>
> *1 Cor. 13:4–7*

It's a massive task to display love in all of these many forms when we are under intense pressure. Most days I don't feel like displaying patience, kindness and not being easily angered. I want to 'wipe the floor', so to speak, with people involved who are blocking our path. I don't much feel like responding to the negativity in love. I am also in danger of being very self-focused because of the battle I'm in and not actually giving much thought to other people. We must strongly guard against neglecting others because we are ourselves having a tough time, and do our best to operate in love.

God's Spirit is always there to help us walk through challenging times in love. Being hopeful, trusting and persevering when it's tough. Not trying to dishonour and wipe the floor with people, but loving them as Jesus himself would. That doesn't mean we don't speak the truth when we need to (Jesus was extremely outspoken at times), but when that's necessary it can still be done with dignity and in love, not in arrogance with the aim of crushing others.

The Bible is so flippin' challenging! It sometimes makes me want to go and live as a nun on a remote island – but then I think I'd probably just start arguing with coconuts so I might as well stay put!

Self-discipline

God's Spirit helps us to be disciplined. Any of us trying to adopt a healthy lifestyle know how difficult self-discipline can be. Getting off the couch to throw some sweaty shapes around the lounge or gym does not come naturally to many of us. But when we do it, it really pays off. Self-discipline is vital to living a life that thrives. If you are in a challenging time, I would say you need to be looking after yourself as well as you can. Exercise, eat nutritious food and enjoy some treats and special times with friends and family too. If we feel sluggish and are full of rubbish food our mind is not in a good state to deal well with the difficulties surrounding our situations. We will be much better equipped if we are getting regular exercise and eating well and feeling sharp both physically and mentally (this book is not being sponsored by Mr Motivator, though if you buy two copies you get a cheeky discount on multi-coloured bum bags – say 'Huh').

We also need to be disciplined in spending time with God. It's very easy for all of us to let this slip, but we must seek God for his perspective and to gain strength to face each day of our battle. We all know it's necessary and important but it's so easy for the days to roll by without talking to God, seeking him and reading his word. We must be hot on this and be self-disciplined. God is ready and waiting and really desires that we spend time with him – he has so much wisdom and encouragement to share with us. But we must choose to tune in.

We must be self-disciplined in our thought lives. So many negative thoughts roll through my mind each day as we await this decision. One minute my faith is sky high as I'm reflecting on God's promises, the next minute I want to cry as it all seems so unlikely to happen. It's pretty tough to do, but we must constantly pull our minds back to his word and his promises. That is the truth in our situation and it must be our main focus.

When a professional involved in our fostering situation sat in front of us and spoke negative things about how unlikely our approval as carers would be, I felt a righteous indignation rising up. I don't honestly fully know what righteous indignation means but I think it sounds really good and I'm pretty sure that is what it was! The Scripture from Hebrews 10:39 that says: 'But we do not belong to those who shrink back and are destroyed, but to those who have faith and are saved' came to my mind. Despite the impossibilities spoken over my personal situation, I am digging my faith heels in and refusing to shrink back.

I do wish my own butt would shrink back a bit though – I'll keep up the squats. Remember – keep your squats low and your standards high.

REFLECTION

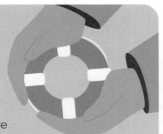

Do you feel brave or timid at the moment?

Reflect on the themes of power, love and self-discipline we have looked at today and do a bit of an evaluation of where you are at with each of them.

Are you eating a healthy balanced diet and taking regular exercise? I'm naturally a salad-dodger (and not a jammy-dodger dodger!), but I do see a real difference in my physical and mental health when I eat better and exercise. Could you make even a few small healthy changes to your lifestyle?

Email me with your multicoloured bum bag orders.

PRAYER

God, today I thank you for your Spirit, who helps us to resist shrinking back in timidity. Naturally speaking, I'm battling with feeling timid due to the challenging situation I'm in. It makes me feel helpless and anxious, but I really desire to move forward in power, love and self-discipline. Thank you that when I feel powerless, it's an opportunity to rely on your power and remind myself that you are influencing this situation in ways I may never even see or know. Help me to look for opportunities to love others, and not to miss people around me who are struggling with their own battles. I want to be a person who is disciplined, and I acknowledge that healthy habits are so important – I ask you to bring to mind things in my life that need to change. I want to take responsibility for my physical, mental, emotional and spiritual health – show me ways I can make adjustments to my life to ensure I'm in the best possible health to go through this challenge as well as I can. Amen.

GOD'S 'BUT' KEEPS ITS EYE ON THE PRIZE

So Jacob served seven years to get Rachel, *but* they seemed like only a few days to him because of his love for her. (Genesis 29:20)

This has got to be one of the most romantic Scriptures ever, it gives me the warm fuzzies – even Hallmark films don't come close to this level of love and romance. I feel I should mention that I'm not in agreement with the way marriage worked back then, in terms of women being worked for or paid for, etc. But from what I can see from this text I feel that regardless of my disapproval of the historical marriage protocol, Jacob was head over heels in love with Rachel, so much so that he was prepared to graft for seven years to be able to marry her. The seven years 'seemed like only a few days to him because of his love for her'. Swoon dot com. His feelings for Rachel were so intense that seven solid years of hard graft felt like just a few days. (I'll be reminding my husband of this story in the future when he moans about the two-minute job of taking the bin out!) No Milk Tray man needed here, Jacob is nailing the passion and romance.

Jacob is actually tricked into marrying Leah, Rachel's sister, first; he then has to work yet another seven years to be able to marry

Rachel. That's some impressive levels of love and commitment, which again will be used as leverage in my marriage – 'So let me get this straight, Jacob grafted fourteen years because he was so in love with Rachel but you don't even love me enough to spend ten seconds putting your undies in the basket?' (Not that I've planned my rants in advance or anything.)

The point I want us to consider from Jacob's story today is that the joy and anticipation of his dream of marrying Rachel made the hard graft of the time in between feel like 'just a few days'. As he was working hard for Laban he must've been dreaming about what married life with Rachel would be like. Planning date nights, imagining their future children, excited to take their bins out (won't mention this again, hubster). Focusing on the life he dreamt of must have kept his spirits up in the difficulties, hard work and monotony of each day during those seven years. Today's 'but' reminds us to keep our levels of hope and excitement up. In focusing on our dream of what life could look like when God 'buts in' and our circumstance shifts, we can have a sense of holy anticipation. Focus your thoughts on the way you and others will be blessed when God turns things around. It will help this time of struggle and hard graft feel sweeter if you do.

Jesus went to the cross with his eyes on the prize – that prize was a relationship with you and me. 'For the joy that was set before him he endured the cross' (Heb. 12:2). It's very humbling to think that Jesus faced the horror of the cross because he wanted our lives and our eternities to be spent with him. Perhaps in order to bless other people, see others healed and helped and our own selves transformed, we have to face a 'seven years of hard graft' Jacob-type season.

These 'seven years of hard graft' times could cause us to back off, check out, think 'forget it, it's too hard believing for a miracle and standing in faith', especially for such a long time. We may fear life continuing to be tense and stressful, or fear risking disappointment, embarrassment or failure. But if we keep our eyes on the prize, on the reason we are believing for this breakthrough, it spurs us on.

You may be praying for a marriage to be restored, or trying to conceive or to get a new job – allow yourself to dream about what that could look like. Be stirred – focus on the joy ahead and the people who could be blessed by you choosing now to stand in faith and to believe in God to do the impossible. Persevere in your present suffering or challenge because of the joy ahead.

I don't find it easy to be optimistic. I can be very cynical and it's a massive effort for me to believe good outcomes are likely or even possible. My husband on the other hand is 'Mr positive pants'. He has a plaque by his bed that says, 'Wake up and be awesome', which makes me want to be a bit sick! Mine has a picture of a crab that says, 'Crabby in the morning'. I really love that about him though; he lives with such a positive outlook and despite my gloomy natural inclinations, I want to learn to do the same. Not in a faux Disney-type 'everything is wonderful and birds are helping me to get dressed' kind of way, but in a way that acknowledges I have a real relationship with Almighty God. That I recognise that God is on my side, therefore I am more than a conqueror. I want to dare to dream and anticipate exciting things to come. I want to daydream like Jacob did of the blessings and 'but ins' to come in the future and for that excitement to take the edge off the tricky times I'm currently facing. For these 'divine daydreams' to give me hope, excitement and anticipation for the future, and the courage to persevere in faith.

Why not be a 'daydream believer' today? Cue song that's now in your head for the rest of the day!

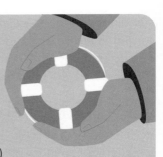

REFLECTION

I would encourage you to spend
some time today thinking about
the future you dream of when this
circumstance you are in shifts, and
to consider those (yourself included)
who will be blessed as a result of it.

Could you place some little reminders of your dream
around your home, maybe a photo or a Scripture, so
when you see them you'll be prompted to keep your eyes
on the prize?

PRAYER

God, please help me to live with a sense of holy anticipation during this testing time. Give me the ability to hope
for a future where this circumstance shifts and where joyful times are ahead. I want to be a 'daydream believer', and
anticipate the good things that will come when you bring
a breakthrough. I pray that my 'seven years of hard labour'
type of season will pass by more sweetly as I do as Jacob
did, and dream about the blessings ahead of me. Help me
to live each day, as mundane as it may be, with courage,
perseverance and an excitement to see what you will do
next. Amen.

GOD'S 'BUT' COVERS OUR WEAKNESSES

But he said to me: 'My grace is sufficient for you, for my power is made perfect in weakness.' (2 Corinthians 12:9)

We were all set on Friday to get the answer we had been waiting for, and then we found out that there would be a further unexpected delay of up to two weeks. Shine on! The friends and family supporting us must be praying hard as we have coped well and had a relatively good weekend despite that news on Friday.

A new challenge has reared its head (oh, joy!) which is that I'm finding it hard to keep my faults and other issues of life in perspective. I keep being drawn in my mind to my failings and mistakes (even dating back to years ago) and they are taunting me in some ways, telling me I don't deserve this breakthrough. My life is not perfect (whose is?) and I'm taking comfort from this Scripture from 2 Corinthians 12:9 which states that God's power is made perfect in our weaknesses.

It is believed that Paul's weakness referred to in this verse was a physical ailment, that God didn't take away despite his pleading. His weakness enabled him to cling on tight to God, to rely on him and his power and not to become a slave to his own ego. God was

119

using Paul powerfully, and the temptation could have been for him to think he was 'all that and a bag of chips'. Our weaknesses, though unpleasant to us, can be used as a vehicle by which we stay grounded, humble, repentant and reliant on God. Paul goes on to say that he even boasts in his weaknesses, as they mean that God's power rests on him.

All of us have pasts packed with highs, lows, joys, challenges, sin and victory. None of us deserve any of God's goodness and grace. So if, like me, you find yourself in a place where you are feeling un-worthy, take heart! If you have genuinely repented of any wrong-doing before God, you are forgiven. Slate wiped completely clean. I love this Scripture from Psalm 103:11–12:

> For as high as the heavens are above the earth,
>   so great is his love for those who fear him;
> as far as the east is from the west,
>   so far has he removed our transgressions from us.

Your sins and mistakes that you have confessed to God are as far away from you as you can possibly imagine. God holds nothing against you. Even better than that, he sees you as completely right and pure before him. This is because Jesus died for all of our sins and weaknesses, he paid the price for it all so we can live free from the weight of guilt and shame caused by our sin.

I am well aware that I am weak, flawed and in need of God's grace every day. This is a good position to be in. I know full well that I've messed up, made mistakes and have ongoing issues in my life that need some serious work. But I also know that I am free in Jesus' name. I am loved, forgiven, treasured and championed by him. I am his child. I want to serve him well and to follow him as best as I can. I believe he wants good things for me. He sees me as a whole – strengths, weaknesses, the whole package – and he loves me.

I'm going to do my best, whenever thoughts of failure come to mind, to replace them with God's truth. Yes, I have sinned and failed, but I have also sincerely asked for his forgiveness and he has forgiven me. There is no need for me to carry guilt, shame and feelings of unworthiness. I need to remain in confident expectation for a 'but in'. Being reminded of my failings is another tactic of the enemy to keep me in fear and defeat and I'm refusing to let him have the victory.

Paul goes on to say, 'Therefore I will boast all the more gladly about my weaknesses, so that Christ's power may rest in me. That is why, for Christ's sake, I delight in weaknesses, in insults, in hardships, in persecutions, in difficulties. For when I am weak, then I am strong' (2 Corinthians 12:9–10).

The Bible is full of paradoxes, and this is a big one – that when we are weak, it's then we are actually strong. We can use our areas of weakness to press more into God, to acknowledge more fully our need for him, and in doing so allow more of his power to rest on us. Let's be thankful for and willingly accepting of his sufficient grace for our weakness, and stand strong as his much-loved children. We are adopted into his family for ever, no mistake would cause him to turn his back on us.

Every night I do a little bedtime speech with my daughter. It's the same every night and she now has it memorised and says and signs it along with me. It goes like this: 'Good night, beautiful girl. I love you, you're my treasure. Sleep well and I'll see you in the morning.' She then gives me a kiss, waves and says, 'Night night, Mummy'. I say, 'Goodnight, old bean' and she replies, 'Goodnight, old bean.' (It's related to Mr Tumble – if you know, you know!) We both then giggle as I end by saying, 'Stay in your bed', and we are laughing as we know that is highly unlikely to happen! The last part of the goodnight speech (yes, I know it goes on a bit!), is: 'You are the apple of my eye, the love of my life, the girl of my dreams – you are my treasure beyond measure.' When I consider how much I love my daughter and the strong and tender feelings I have for her, it's really nothing compared to how God feels about us. He loves us deeply, passionately, perfectly – more than we can comprehend.

My daughter is adopted – this means she is fully a legal member of our family. She is cherished, loved, accepted and wanted as much as if I had given birth to her – I have no doubt of that. If we are believers then we have been adopted into God's family. It's not a temporary status based on how well we have or haven't performed. It's a permanent legal change of status. He is our good father and we are the children who he loves. Fully fledged members of his forever family. Warts and all, we are eternally his. Nothing can separate us from his incredible love (Rom. 8:39).

Don't let your weaknesses and mistakes make you feel disqualified from receiving God's promises. He knows we are weak and that we mess up. Confess anything to him that is on your mind and move forward, knowing you are unconditionally accepted and loved.

I'm reminded of an old hymn called 'Before the Throne of God Above' which contains so many powerful truths – this is one of the verses that's particularly apt for today:

> When Satan tempts me to despair,
> and tells me of the guilt within
> upward I look and see him [Jesus] there,

who made an end to all my sin.
Because the sinless Saviour died,
my sinful soul is counted free,
for God the just is satisfied
to look on him and pardon me.

Receive that truth today. Yes, we should want to live lives that honour and please our Father God. But the reality is that we will continue to fail and make mistakes. Own up to them, confess them and leave them with him – because he throws them into the sea to be gone for ever and there's no need for us to go fishing for them.

You will again have compassion on us;
you will tread our sins underfoot
and hurl our iniquities into the depths of the sea.

Mic. 7:19

REFLECTION

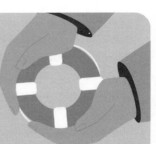

Have you experienced failures from the past trying to bite you in the butt?

How do you feel reflecting on the fact that you are a child of God, adopted into his family for ever?

What do you think about the verse from Micah about our sins being hurled into the depths of the sea? Are you ever tempted to go fishing for them?

Say 'Goodnight, old bean' to someone this evening and see how that goes down.

PRAYER

God, I'm so humbled by your goodness, kindness, mercy and forgiveness. I admit that I have failed you so many times, and I have areas of my life and character that need a lot of work. I'm so grateful that Jesus died to pay for all of my sin. I stand as a completely forgiven person because of the cross. Beyond that amazing truth, you also call me your adopted child – I am forever yours, a beloved member of your family. Thank you that you accept me, love me and are so patient with me despite the many times I fail you. I choose to focus today on the amazingly gracious way you deal with my sins – you hurl them into the sea and you never go fishing for them. Help me to accept this incredible gift and to stand against any lies that tell me I'm not good enough. You don't want me to live in guilt and shame, so today I choose to live in the freedom you died to give to me. Thank you for your unconditional love to me, and the security and assurance I have in being called your child. Amen.

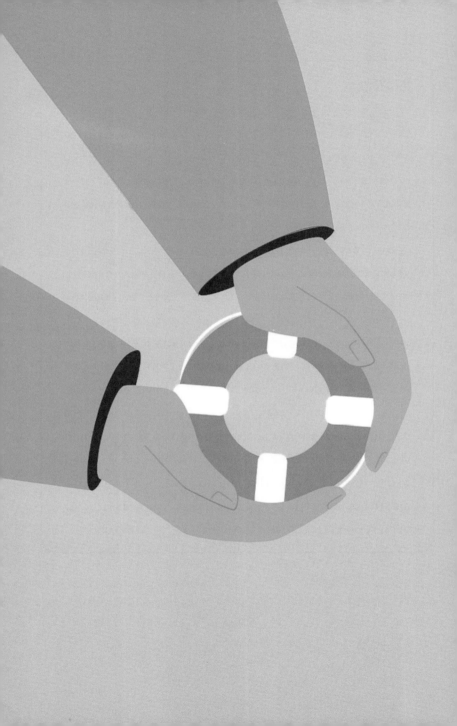

GOD'S 'BUT' SHIELDS US

But you, LORD, are a shield around me, my glory, the One who lifts my head high. (Psalm 3:3)

Psalm 3 is a short but very powerful psalm. It's so short that I'll quote all eight verses in full:

> LORD, how many are my foes!
>> How many rise up against me!
> Many are saying of me,
>> 'God will not deliver him.'
>
> But you, LORD, are a shield around me,
>> my glory, the One who lifts my head high.
> I call out to the LORD,
>> and he answers me from his holy mountain.
>
> I lie down and sleep;
>> I wake again because the LORD sustains me.
> I will not fear though tens of thousands
>> assail me on every side.

Arise, LORD!
  Deliver me, my God!
Strike all my enemies on the jaw;
  break the teeth of the wicked.

From the LORD comes deliverance.
  May your blessing be on your people.

The context for David writing this psalm is a time of intense trouble. His son Absalom was leading a rebellion against him which was proving to be successful. Not only was his own son rebelling against him, but people who had previously supported David were now saying that God would not deliver him. Talk about a slap in the face, on so many levels. Friends and family are completely against him, people are speaking hopelessness and defeat over him.

Yet David is encouraged. He doesn't get knocked off track by the many serious troubles and disappointments he is facing. He boldly declares that God is his shield, his protection. He doesn't ask God to be his shield, he states that God is his shield – it's a given for David that God will protect him. David knows God so intimately that he completely trusts him to keep him safe and secure in the midst of incredibly challenging times.

A shield is a person or thing giving protection, from danger, risk or unpleasant experience. David knew God was his personal shield. In Psalm 7:10 he says, 'My shield is God Most High.'

My situation is nowhere near on the same scale as David's, but I feel like I have sensed God's shielding power within our challenge. I have experienced in the last few months significant protection over my mind, heart and emotions. We have had every reason to feel discouraged, dejected and rejected. But largely I haven't felt that. I've certainly had to do some hard work in this area myself and keep bringing myself back to God's word, worshipping him and fixing my mind on him. But I honestly think God must have done some supernatural shielding for us to remain at this level of peace and calm throughout the past few challenging months. I think our prayers, and the prayers of friends and family, have in some way activated God's shielding power over our lives. We have prayed that professionals involved will take note of how calm we've been throughout and that this will reflect God's goodness in our lives to them.

I really love how David goes on in Psalm 3 to say that God is his glory and the lifter of his head. God doesn't just protect and shield him in the trial, but he lifts him up. He helps David to be secure and hold his head high, despite the rejection of many people and the many enemies seeking to destroy him. Even in the middle of this terrible situation, God empowers him, gives him boldness and confidence that he will deliver him. David is a man of impressive faith, expectation and intimacy with God.

God's 'but' is there to shield us in times of trouble.

> The LORD is a refuge for the oppressed,
>> a stronghold in times of trouble.
> Those who know your name trust in you,
>> for you, LORD, have never forsaken those who seek you.
>
> *Ps. 9:9–10*

If you are feeling rejected, oppressed, downtrodden or discouraged, get yourself behind God's shielding 'but'. Not only will he cover and protect you, but he will also lift up your head.

REFLECTION

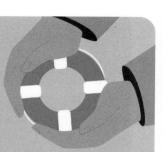

Thank God that he acts as a shield of protection over you. In what ways do you feel you need his shielding protection? Mentally? Emotionally? Spiritually? Physically? In which of these areas do you feel you have or are experiencing this shielding?

Reflect on the part of our verse for today that says God delivers us and lifts up our head. What does that mean to you and how can this encourage you in your current situation?

Do you feel that you are able to hold your head high as a child of God despite the challenging circumstances you are in? If not, spend some time in prayer and ask God to help you to hold your head high and to stand strong in your identity in him.

PRAYER

God, I'm encouraged by David's example of confidence in your ability to shield and protect him from trouble. He was going through an exceptionally difficult time, yet he knew you were the faithful one he could run to for strength and protection. Not only did he know you would shield him, but he also says that you are the lifter of his head. God, when people are against me, I can stand firm in the truth that you are for me, you are championing me and you lift my head so I can go through the test with dignity and courage. Thank you that you are a shield, a refuge, and a stronghold I can always run to in times of trouble. Amen.

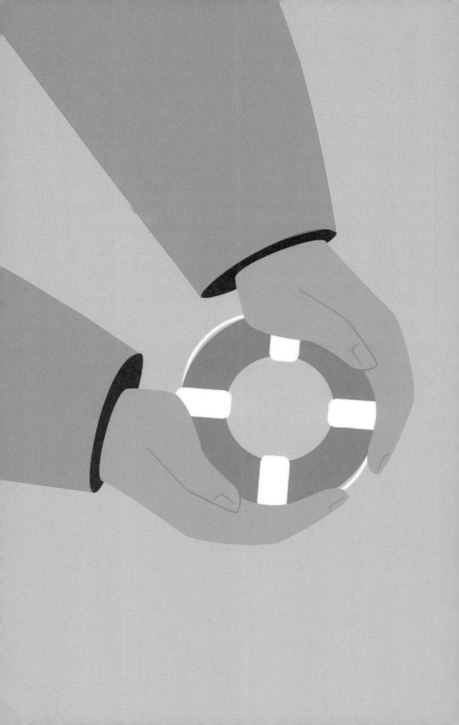

GOD'S 'BUT' IS FIRMLY PLANTED

When the storm has swept by, the wicked are gone, *but* the righteous stand firm forever . . . the righteous will never be uprooted. (Proverbs 10:25,30)

Today's 'but' brings a challenge for us to stand firm, to stand tough, to stand our ground. During our impossible-seeming situations, I want to encourage us to be firm in our convictions and resilient against opposition. The roots of our faith need to grow down deeply to steady us in this testing time. When we are believing in God to do something that humanly feels impossible, it's probable that many storm-like conditions will attempt to destabilise us.

With this in mind, I want to challenge us today to become like . . . wait for it . . . weeds. Yes, you read it right – God needs more weeds (makes for a great hashtag!). I know in Christian literature you'd normally be encouraged to become like a beautiful sunflower pointing heavenward. Nope, no time for the sunflower analogy here today. You may be thinking, but weeds are awful, you just can't get rid of them. Well, that's my point exactly. Weeds are hardy, they are stubborn, they're defiant even.

Last year I had a real grass disaster. I think it's fair to say I went a little OTT with the weed-killer on our back lawn (which shameful-ly was approx. 50 per cent weeds and 50 per cent grass). To my horror, I soon discovered that I had used the wrong kind of weed-killer – one you don't use anywhere near grass. I literally killed off (the other) half of our lawn. A local gardener came to assess the situation. (He was recommended by a friend whose approval was largely based on the fact he had a slogan T-shirt that said, 'I'm sexy and I mow it' – a good enough endorsement for me.) He surveyed my dry and barren land and concluded in his strong Yorkshire ac-cent: 'Yep, you've defo gone pretty mental wit' weed-killer, 'aven't you.' However, with his advice I managed to grow my grass back and I'm now a proud lawn-again Christian.

In my defence, weeds are notoriously difficult to get rid of. If you've ever attempted to dig one of the blighters up, you'll know how deep and chunky their roots can be. They ain't going nowhere fast. If weeds could talk, I imagine they'd have a Phil Mitchell-style voice. If you could humour me and say, 'Oi, Titchmarsh – come and have a go if you think you're hard enough' out loud in an aggres-sive cockney accent I'm sure you'll see what I mean. (Make sure you aren't in public for this exercise.)

I believe we need to develop this hardy, weed-like spirit as the in-evitable challenges come towards us. If we truly believe that God has spoken, we need to be firmly planted in his promises. 1 Corin-thians 15:58 says: 'Stand firm. Let nothing move you.' Let's develop a 'stubborn stability' because we trust completely in the reliability of God's word to us. Let's decide to dig in, and to dig down deep. To be firmly planted. To be defiant in the face of challenges. To not go down without a fight – to be tenacious and aggressive against fear and doubt that will seek to uproot us.

Sometimes we can be so feeble; I know that's certainly true of myself at times. I look at scary realities around me and I can be blown away as easily as a fluffy dandelion. We need to remember that we have Almighty God on our side. We aren't being arrogant in adopting our steadfast position, as our solid roots are not linked to our own ability or power. Our roots can be sturdy and secure because in God we are 'more than conquerors'. Each time we speak out or reflect on God's word our roots grow down a bit deeper. Feed yourself with faith today – develop some thick roots to anchor you in the storm – alongside developing that aggressive cockney accent of course!

Let's join together as a band of weeds and sing, 'Weeds shall not, weeds shall not be moved'. Be firmly planted in your convictions today and in your belief for God to 'but in' and do the impossible – and remember as you do this, 'The righteous will never be uprooted.'

#Godneedsmoreweeds #weedsshallnotbemoved

REFLECTION

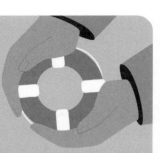

Are you more fluffy dandelion
or hardy weed at the moment?

Can you think of a better voice for a
weed than Phil Mitchell's? Please do
let me know if so.

Do you need to develop more of a tenacious and steadfast spirit in the storms that come your way?

PRAYER

God, I'm grateful for your word that says, 'The righteous will never be uprooted'. I want to be a person who stands firm in the middle of the inevitable storms of life. I want to develop resilience, and a 'stubborn stability' as I navigate this difficult season. Thank you that I can be sturdy and stable because I'm rooted in your truth and love. Help me to be like a hardy weed, tenacious and thick-rooted, and to resist my tendency towards being blown by the wind like a fluffy dandelion seed. Remind me that you say I am more than a conqueror, and help me to encourage my fellow band of weeds to stand firm in you too. Amen.

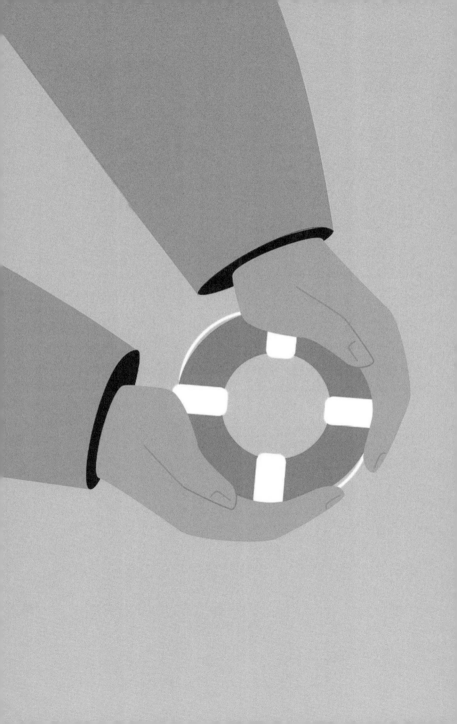

GOD'S 'BUT' GETS TO THE HEART OF THE MATTER

Likewise, the tongue is a small part of the body, *but* it makes great boasts. Consider what a great forest is set on fire by a small spark. (James 3:5)

The words we speak over ourselves and others carry more power than we often realise. As today's 'but' states – the tongue may be a small part of your body but it makes 'great boasts'. The passage goes on to say some strong things about the power of the tongue: 'The tongue also is a fire, a world of evil among the parts of the body. It corrupts the whole body, sets the whole course of one's life on fire, and is itself set on fire by hell' (Jas 3:6).

This is extremely strong language to describe the power such a small part of us can have. If we do not control our tongue, the evil and destruction it can cause is severe.

I've been reading quite a bit of the 'Emotionally Healthy Discipleship' material by Pete Scazzero recently; I highly recommend it.[2] One of the sections encourages readers to 'go back to go forward' – meaning, to think about your past experiences that may still be impacting you now, in order to deal with them and be enabled to move forward positively from them. In doing this I have realised that some unkind things said to me in my early teenage years have significantly impacted me – much more than I had realised. One particular comment – where someone said I was ugly compared to pretty girls I spent a lot of time with – I can now see has really stuck and negatively impacted my self-esteem for most of my life. I'm glad I've recently been able to identify the root of the battle I've continuously faced in not feeling attractive enough or good enough and comparing myself with others. I hope now that I'm aware of this, I can reach a place of freedom and healing. I think this will take time and I'm having some professional counselling too – I want to do whatever it takes to not be held back by this any longer.

The point of me sharing that story is not to make you feel sorry for me (though if you get the urge to send sympathy chocolates then who am I to stop a kind deed – I like Toblerone). As a side note, Toblerone is a very spiritual choice of chocolate as it's triangular in shape with three points representing the Trinity. (I can find a spiritual link to any chocolate I fancy – it's a real gift of mine!) I really hope that the experience I've shared with you from my younger years highlights how one particularly negative and hurtful comment can have a powerful impact on a person's life for many years. We can affect people's lives for years to come for good or for bad. We can use our tongue to speak words of life, hope and encouragement, or we can use it to insult, discourage and tear people down.

In relation to our impossible situations, I want us to reflect on the words that are currently coming out of our mouths. How are you speaking about your situation today? Are you speaking about the reality of the situation along with words of life, faith, hope and positivity? Or are you speaking the reality of what you see along with gloom, fear, doubt and negativity? Challenging times make me realise how inclined I am to think negatively and expect the worst. Doubt and fear come much more naturally to me than faith and expectation. I know this because of the way I speak about tough times. I'm doing my best to change that trend.

In Proverbs 18:21 the Bible says that 'the tongue has the power of life and death'. That's another strong statement which we must pay attention to. It shows how incredibly important and significant the words that come from our mouths are. We have the ability to speak life or death over ourselves, over other people and over our circumstances.

I don't believe it's as simple as learning a set of chirpy positive phrases and thinking if we repeat them parrot fashion twenty times a day then everything will work out swell! 'You got this', 'positive vibes' and 'yasss queen' will only get you so far! We need to be speaking out words of real power and substance – which are the promises of God that we find in the Bible.

What comes out of our mouths actually originates in our hearts: 'A good person produces good things from the treasury of a good heart, and an evil person produces evil things from the treasury of an evil heart. What you say flows from what is in your heart' (Luke 6:45, NLT).

The Bible is clear that it's not simply about changing the words we speak. We need to ensure the condition of our heart is good, as that's where what comes out of our mouths actually originates.

If in our heart we are seeking God, doing our best to trust him, earnestly praying and reflecting on his reliability and miraculous power, then what we say about our situation is likely to be faith-filled and hopeful. But if our hearts are full of darkness, doubt, disappointment, bitterness and hopelessness then our confession will follow along those negative lines. We cannot just trot out shallow statements, however positive they may be; we need a deep and lasting work done in our heart, and that comes from knowing God, knowing his word, trusting his character and growing in confidence in who he is.

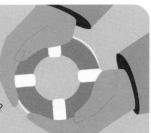

REFLECTION

Has anyone ever said anything to
you that has stuck with you and
impacted you either for good or bad?

How will recognising this affect how
you speak to yourself and to others
from now on?

How will today's 'but' change the way you speak to others
about difficulties they are experiencing?

Do you think you mainly speak positively or negatively
about your challenge?

If you are really brave, ask someone close to you what
they think about the above question.

On a scale of 1 to 10, how moved do you feel to send me a
Toblerone?

Can you make a spiritual link to your favourite snack? FYI
they make giant Toblerone – go big or go home I say.

PRAYER

God, I ask you to bring to mind any words that have been spoken over me that have in any way damaged or negatively affected me. I ask you to begin a work of healing in my life. I know this is a process that takes time, but I'm committed to gaining freedom from anything spoken over me that is holding me back. I really want the words I speak over myself, other people and my current challenge to be full of genuine hope, faith and life. I acknowledge today the power of the tongue, and I understand from your word that what comes out of my mouth is a reflection of what is happening in my heart. Show me the areas of my heart that need to be transformed – where there is darkness, bitterness, sadness and disappointment, I pray you would begin to highlight those things to me. Thank you for your grace, kindness and patience towards me as I work through these difficult issues. Amen.

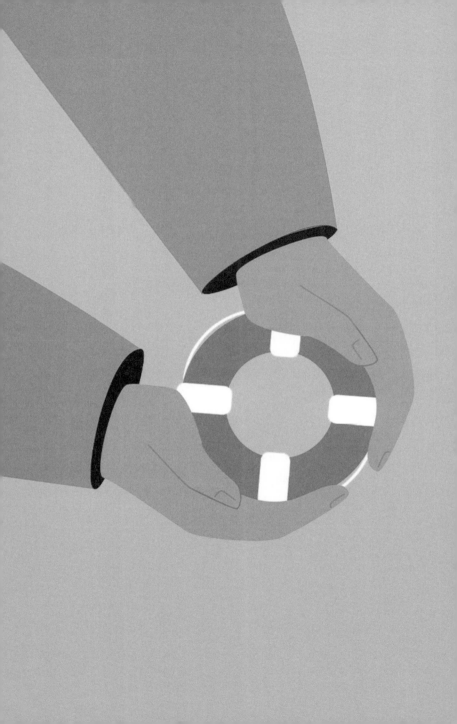

GOD'S 'BUT' IS NOT SURPRISED BY SUFFERING

**Dear friends, do not be surprised at the fiery ordeal that has
come on you to test you, as though something strange were
happening to you. *But* rejoice inasmuch as you participate in
the sufferings of Christ, so that you may be overjoyed when
his glory is revealed. (1 Peter 4:12–13)**

Well, this is an intense start to today's devotion! I love Scriptures
about God's promises to protect, provide for and sustain me. The
one I've chosen for today is not particularly easy to stomach. It's
not a passage we often share when others are in a difficult situation, or when we ourselves are walking through a challenging
time. I prefer the 'rising up on eagles' wings' type of verses to a 'rejoicing in suffering' Scripture! Yet it's extremely important that we
grasp the hard truths communicated by the words of Peter. Let's
reflect on two nuggets of hard truth from todays 'but' passage.

'Do not be surprised'

The Bible is not a fluffy book. It certainly contains loads of wisdom
and encouragement but that stands alongside many hard truths.
It explicitly tells us not to be surprised when we experience tough
and testing times. They should not be viewed by us as strange

times, but as an integral part of our journey of life and faith in Jesus. When we read the Bible, it is far from trouble-free. We don't see the disciples swanning around from one miracle to the next being showered with praise, money and any other material thing they could possibly desire. The lives of believers in Scripture were characterised by a whole mixture of trials and triumphs, faith and fear, laughter and lament. Yet despite knowing that, when trials come our way, we can often still feel a bit put out, cheesed off, and even offended that God would allow any sort of negative experience to come our way. I've certainly had my fair share of Kevin the teenager's 'this is so unfair' style strops at God when I have faced difficult times. Yet God clearly states that trials will come, it's certainly no secret that's the case. We shouldn't need Cilla Black to shout, 'Surprise, surprise, it's a fiery trial', as we shouldn't be surprised at all. Experiencing a trial does not signal that God has left you, is angry with you or has removed his favour or protection from you. It is a normal and inevitable part of living the life of faith. Your faith will be tested. We need to remember that whatever the trial or circumstance, God never leaves us; we face no trial alone (Heb. 13:5).

Rejoice in your sufferings

Wait, what? Does God know that to rejoice means 'to feel joy or great delight'? Surely, he can't expect me to be joyful and delighting in the fact that a decision of whether I can do something I really feel him calling me to is hanging in the balance? Surely he can't expect me to be 'blessed not stressed' when things that are happening are so frustrating and beyond my control? How can he want me to be happy and joyful when life is painful, uncertain and challenging? We need to keep in mind that our faith is counter-cultural. Our western culture says that we can be happy, delighting and joyful when we hit a list of ideals like having a well-paid job, a nice house or car, an attractive partner on our arm, full health, white teeth and toned buns. If we can tick several or all of those boxes and we are not experiencing any pain or challenge then we can be happy, content and winning in life. We need to be careful as Christ followers that we don't subscribe to those cultural ideals. The word of God needs to be our standard for life, not the word of the Kardashians (complete with their toned buns) or whoever else may be in favour in popular culture (I'm 38 and the fact that I've just used the phrase 'popular culture' makes me feel at least 108!). In James 1:2–4 it says: 'Consider it pure joy, my brothers and sisters, whenever you face trials of many kinds, because you know the testing of your faith produces perseverance. Let perseverance finish its work so that you may be mature and complete, not lacking anything.'

I have to admit that I'm often more interested in Percy Pigs than I am in good old Percy Verance! (Probably the reason my buns are untoned!)

Today, can we try our best to view our impossible situations and the challenges that come along with them differently? Could we dare to thank God for the opportunity to know him more deeply because of them? To seek him harder, to begin to see the fruit of perseverance and maturity in our lives? To reject the world's standards of happiness, and to embrace suffering and challenge as Jesus himself did? Can we allow God to do a deep work in us and resist the often shallow values our culture says are the standard to live by?

REFLECTION

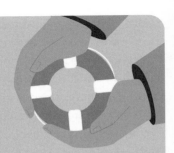

When your current trial entered your life how did you feel? Angry at God? Surprised? Confused? Cheesed off? Joyful?

Do you feel like it's possible for you to remain joyful in the middle of this difficult time?

I definitely recommend you treat yourself to a bag of Percy Pigs today, and I hope whenever you see them in future, you'll be reminded that we need to Percy-vere in trials. Call it a 'confection reflection'. 'Deep' is my middle name!

PRAYER

God, today's theme of being joyful in suffering is such a difficult one to get my head around. Your word is not always easy to understand or to live out, and rejoicing in suffering is certainly not my natural inclination. I want to be shaped by the values of your kingdom, as opposed to the often shallow ideals of the culture I'm living in. Help me to embrace what your word says about not being surprised by suffering. Remind me, when I feel annoyed that what I'm experiencing feels unfair, that you and your followers faced many trials. None of us on this planet is immune to suffering. I want to learn to persevere during difficult times, and do my best to rejoice throughout them. I have a lot to learn in this area, but I want to go through and grow through suffering in a way that honours you. Amen.

THINGS CHANGE DRAMATICALLY WHEN GOD'S 'BUT' IS IN THE BOAT

When he had finished speaking, he said to Simon, 'Put out into deep water, and let down the nets for a catch.' Simon answered, 'Master, we've worked hard all night and haven't caught anything. *But* because you say so, I will let down the nets.' (Luke 5:4–5)

Imagine you are Peter. You have been slogging your guts out all night on your boat, desperately trying to catch some fish. It's your livelihood – to put it simply, you need dem krill to pay dem bills. This is not a hobby – your family are depending on the income these fish will supply, you are under a huge amount of pressure to see the goods surface. After a highly unsuccessful night, I imagine Peter would be feeling deflated, exhausted, hungry, hangry and hopeless.

Jesus comes along and first of all asks to use Peter's boat to preach from (which doesn't seem to be the most sensitive request in the middle of Peter's fishless frenzy). After he finishes preaching, Jesus asks Peter to let down his net – again. Peter's response really impresses me. He respectfully addresses Jesus as 'Master' and he acknowledges the reality that they have been up all chuffin' night trying to catch fish with no success. But he ends by saying, 'But because you say so, I will let down the nets.' Often people who are in authority use the phrase, 'Because I say so' when they are asked the question, 'Why?' Jesus didn't have this kind of authoritarian attitude, and it's evident that Peter recognised and submitted to Jesus' authority out of his own choice. Peter didn't ask Jesus 'why?', instead he just obeyed and said, 'Because you say so.'

Peter saw in Jesus someone who was worth trusting against all cods (sorry, against all odds). In Peter's mind he knew there was no chance of any fish being caught when he had already spent a full night trawling, but even at this early stage in their relationship he seemed to grasp how special and important Jesus was, and this was enough to cause Peter to obey Jesus' strange and confusing command.

I am doing my best to learn from Peter's trust and obedience in this situation. When what we are facing seems bleak and hopeless, when we feel similar to Peter in that we've been grafting all night with no breakthrough, that's when Jesus often shows up. But it's more than him just showing up; we need to act on his word to us. We need to obey him and trust him when nothing he says or asks of us really makes sense, and especially when we just do not feel like it.

What might God be asking you to obey today that in honesty, you just don't feel like obeying? What does God ask of you that feels the opposite of what you want to do or what feels logical to do? Here are a few Scriptures and examples that I feel may be relevant:

- 'Do not become weary in doing good, for at the proper time you will reap a harvest if you do not give up' (Gal. 6:9). Maybe you do feel extremely weary, and yet God is asking you to resist weariness and to keep cracking on.
- 'Trust in the LORD with all of your heart

and lean not on your own understanding;
in all your ways submit to him,
        and he will make your paths straight.' (Prov. 3:5–6)
Maybe God is asking you to choose trust today when everything
within you feels let down, disappointed and uncertain.
- 'Do not fear, for I have redeemed you;
        I have summoned you by name, you are mine.' (Isa. 43:1)
Perhaps choosing not to fear today seems totally counterintui-
tive due to the anxiety-inducing circumstances surrounding you.
- 'Give thanks in all circumstances; for this is God's will for you in
Christ Jesus' (1 Thess. 5:18). Maybe thankfulness is not exactly at
the top of your list today, and expressing gratitude to God is the
last thing you want to do.

God does not always ask easy and reasonable-sounding things of
us. Following him means obeying and trusting when we feel like
doing the polar opposite.

I think looking at what happened as a result of Peter's radical obedience will encourage us today: 'When they had done so, they
caught such a large number of fish that their nets began to break'
(Luke 5:6).

If Jesus asks you to 'let down' he will never let you down!

You will (brace yourself) rake in the hake, have breams beyond
your wildest dreams, acquire grace with your plaice, you'll thank
God for your cod, raise a joyful shout with your trout! (Have you
grown to love my humour yet?)

When we recognise that Jesus is Lord, when we acknowledge that
he has command over creation and when we submit to his word,
he will bring blessing and breakthrough to our lives.

So today I want to encourage us to 'go again' – to hang on a bit longer in faith for God to 'but in'. We may feel as though it's over, that the provision, answer or breakthrough will never come – but let's choose obedience as Peter did and choose to 'go again' – to let down our net again, to pray again, serve again, declare again, thank him again, believe again.

REFLECTION

Today, in your personal situation, ask God what it looks like for you to 'go again' like Peter did. Is there a particular Scripture he is highlighting to you today as a personal command to you? Spend some time quietly before him listening to his word to you today.

Did I miss any obvious fish puns? Please get your skate(s) on and email to let me know if so.

PRAYER

God, I'm really challenged by Peter's attitude of trust in you against all odds. After working so hard all night, he was still willing to obey you and to 'go again' even though it must've felt like a pointless exercise. He knew that you were someone worth listening to and trusting in. Thank you for the miracle you did in this impossible-looking situation, and the encouragement that is to me right now in what I'm facing. Give me eyes of faith to see my circumstances in light of what you can do, even when it seems highly unlikely that anything could change. Give me the determination to go again and to not give up hope. Help me, as an act of faith, to do the opposite of what I humanly feel like doing in my situation. Help me to trust again, hope again, believe again. Amen.

GOD'S 'BUT' IS SOLID AS A ROCK

**Do not be overcome by evil, *but* overcome evil with good.
(Romans 12:21)**

I have to admit that I feel increasingly overwhelmed by the evil I see in the world. I turn on the news and hear story after story of utterly desperate situations. Crime, war, relationships breaking down, natural disasters – so many people are hurting and are experiencing the effects of life in a fallen and sinful world. The constant bombardment of bad news is tough, painful, disheartening and depressing. It's so difficult to wrap our brains around the issues of evil and suffering. We live in this strange middle ground where Jesus has won our freedom, but we continue to live in a world full of evil and sin and we are not immune from its effects. We are also not immune from causing its effects ourselves if we are not careful. We wrestle with sin personally and communally. We know in the end that God will fully rule and that we will rule with him. But how do we cope with evil and injustice in the meantime? How do we live in this world effectively and make a difference when we are so choked by the evil we see and experience?

I love how real and raw the Bible is – it's full of wonderfully flawed humans. Take the incredible prophet Elijah as an example – one minute he's brave and bold, calling down fire from heaven in front of the prophets of Baal. The next minute he's sobbing under a tree – terrified, knackered and depressed. We are in good company with the biblical characters – life was not rosy for them and it ain't rosy for us. Some days the news we hear isn't all bad, the people we love are relatively OK and things seem fairly sweet. Other times, it seems like everyone we know is in the middle of a horrendously difficult time and we do feel swamped and overwhelmed.

If you are reading this devotional it's likely that you have chosen to do so because, like me, you are facing a difficult situation. You may be experiencing the effects of evil. Maybe you are experiencing injustice, misrepresentation, betrayal, physical pain, heartache, disappointment, the potential loss of a dream. So how does God tell us to respond? He says to not be overcome by evil, but to overcome evil with good. I love this so much, it really helps me to get some fighting spirit back when I feel down and helpless – both about myself and what is happening in the wider world. It reminds me that I don't have to remain in a state of passive despair, but I can take back some control and choose to do something good to counteract the evil that is at work. It may not be that I can do anything big to improve some of the terrible things that happen. But I do have the power to 'but in' to someone else's life in a positive way and encourage someone every single day of my life. I can send an email to thank someone for their hard work. I can text someone a quote from Scripture and tell them I am praying for them. I can cook someone a meal, I can do something good, no matter how small. In doing so, I take back some of the ground that evil has tried to capture.

I love how Mother Teresa reportedly said, 'Not everyone can do great things, but everyone can do small things with great love.' I honestly believe that acts of love and goodness, as small and insignificant as they may feel to us, have real power over evil. It helps us to recognise that while we can't control and solve so many things, we can choose to continue to be God's agents of love and goodness.

Consider today what you have control over in your situation. You may not have much control at all, but it's likely that you do have control in the following ways: control over your response to the injustice and evil you are experiencing, control over your attitude to the difficulty you are walking through and control over the words that come out of your mouth. Determine today to fix your thoughts and attention on these things you can control and to look for ways, however small, to demonstrate God's goodness and love to others. Refuse to let evil swamp and overwhelm you, but join with the band of rough-and-ready believers we read of in the Bible, whose lives were far from easy, but whose examples we can look to when evil and pain feel overwhelming.

I want to briefly look at two examples of characters in the Bible who looked to God as their rock in times of evil, danger and struggle.

> From the ends of the earth I call to you,
>> I call as my heart grows faint;
>> lead me to the rock that is higher than I.
> For you have been my refuge,
>> a strong tower against the foe.

How incredible are these words of David in Psalm 61? He describes God as his rock – a rock is a picture of the security he feels in God. Describing God as a rock acknowledges that God is his foundation, his hiding-place from the enemy, his refuge, his protector. We un-doubtedly have an enemy causing much evil in this world. In our impossible situations we may be impacted by various aspects of evil right now. Let's look to David's example and remind ourselves that God is our rock – our sure and solid foundation in times of trouble. We can remain grounded in him despite the uncertainty and instability of the circumstances around us.

Then there is Hannah, who said, 'There is no Rock like our God' (1 Sam. 2:2). Hannah had been through the pain of barrenness and a desperate longing for a child. In time God gave her a son whom she called Samuel and she dedicated him back to serve God in the temple. Hannah praises God and, like David, uses the rock metaphor – showing that God is steady, can be relied upon and he is always dependable. In an increasingly uncertain, unsteady, disappointing and evil world, let us join with Hannah and David, viewing God as our rock. 'He will be the sure foundation for your times' (Isa. 33:6).

When evil is overwhelming, let's run to the rock (definitely make sure it's Jesus though, and not Dwayne Johnson), and be determined to engage in acts of goodness and love no matter how insignificant they seem to us. Let God's rock-solid 'but' help you to kick evil in the butt. Be determined to overcome evil with good in any way you can.

REFLECTION

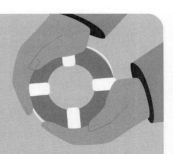

Is there a small act of goodness you can do today? Ask God to bring someone to your mind to do something kind for today.

Spend some time in silence and reflect on the 'rock' metaphor – in what ways has God been your rock when you look back at your life so far?

What can you learn from the examples of David and Hannah and their response to the evil and struggles they faced?

PRAYER

God, when I see the many effects of evil happening around me and in the wider world I feel so down and overwhelmed. Many people are experiencing pain in so many difficult ways and I feel helpless to do anything about it. I'm grateful for inspirational people like Mother Teresa who impacted the world significantly through simple acts of kindness and goodness. Help me to be determined to do the same, to 'overcome evil with good' in any way I can. I'm encouraged today from reflecting on the analogy of you being my rock – you are strong, steady, dependable, and a solid foundation to build my life upon. When I feel wobbly and uncertain, I will echo the words of David: 'Lead me to the rock that is higher than I.' Amen.

GOD'S 'BUT' REFUSES TO SIT IN FEAR

For if you remain silent at this time, relief and deliverance for the Jews will arise from another place, but you and your father's family will perish. And who knows *but* that you have come to your royal position for such a time as this? (Esther 4:14)

The story of Esther is incredible! What a hero of faith she was. Esther did not have an easy upbringing. Both of her parents died and so her uncle Mordecai adopted her and brought her up as his own daughter. I'd really encourage you to read the ten chapters of Esther in full as it's such an exciting, amazing, faith-building read! I'll try and summarise the story extremely briefly – here is 'Esther in a nutshell' the NKWV (the New Kate Williams version – probably not quite as reliable as other versions!).

King Xerxes is cheesed off with his queen who refuses to parade herself round at one of his showy banquets (I'm #TeamVashti on this point to be fair). Xerxes does an *X Factor*-style 'Find me a new beautiful virgin wife' contest and Esther wins. She keeps the fact that she's a Jew secret. Her uncle Mordecai wins some kudos with King X Factor for uncovering a plot to kill him. There's an evil bloke called Haman (not someone you could do a 'hay man' name joke to) who hates the Jews and convinces King X Factor to sign a decree to kill all of the Jews in Persia. Esther asks the Jews to fast and pray and decides to go in to ask the king to reconsider. Haman is unaware of this and has gallows built to hang Mordecai on. The king wakes one night and remembers Mordecai was once involved in preventing his murder. Esther goes into the king, knowing it could result in her death as you strictly (wouldn't be fair not to mention this reality show too) had to be summoned to talk with the king. The king is favourable to her and in the end the Jews are spared. Mordecai is promoted and 'Hay man' is hanged on the gallows he had made for Mordecai.

Esther was an incredible woman of faith – a normal girl from a tough background, yet a real gutsy queen. She totally understood the consequences of going to speak to the king without being summoned by him. But she didn't let fear stop her acting on behalf of the Jewish people. 'When this is done, I will go to the king, even though it is against the law. And if I perish, I perish' (4:16). She knew her bold actions could result in her own death, but she proceeded in bravery and boldness – she didn't sit in fear, she walked in faith. She certainly felt and acknowledged the fear, but she didn't let it rule or overwhelm her.

The book of Esther is a great encouragement to us in the importance of courage and faith, but also in needing the foundations of spiritual disciplines like prayer and fasting to be part of our lives and faith journeys. During our own impossible situation, my husband and I decided to fast once a week. I hadn't fasted for a long time so I decided to start small and fast my lunch once a week – and to ensure I spent time in prayer with my husband too. Not a huge sacrifice in the big scheme of life, but I believe this made a difference – going without food for a time shows God we are serious about seeking and hearing from him. Bringing things to him in prayer is so important, and that regular slot of doing that each week helped me and my husband stand together through the challenge. It helped us to keep God at the centre of our situation, recognising that only he had the power to 'but in' and shift the circumstances we were up against.

One thing I've been reflecting on recently is the level of faith I see in older Christians. We have a lovely friend called Gwen who is 94 and is currently in hospital with a body that is full of cancer. She has been told that she has a couple of weeks left to live. We don't live close by but fortunately my husband was able to visit her in hospital this week. Despite what she is experiencing she remains full of wit and humour, is as sassy and strong-willed as ever; she's cheerful, hopeful and confident in a loving God. I believe this is the case because the foundations of her life of faith are solid. She has spent hours upon hours of her life reading and studying God's word. She has faithfully prayed, fasted and spent regular quality time with God. These spiritual disciplines mean that she can face this difficult time with faith and not fear, much like Esther did.

Without the foundations of these spiritual disciplines, being brave and bold may still be commended, but I don't believe it's anywhere near as effective. The combination of building your life on the spiritual disciplines often modelled by the older generation of Christians, coupled with a commitment to walking in faith and not fear, means you can face difficult times with courage because you have a deep and solid relationship with God.

When I compare the way I respond to challenges in life to the way my friend Gwen is responding to her situation, I see a real disparity. I am often so angry at God for what I'm facing, or I'm weak and 'why me dot com'. I want to look at the examples of both Gwen and Esther – two people who were confident in the power of God, but who also took seriously the importance of putting in the hard work of developing their relationships with God. These women inspire me to evaluate my life and make changes to what gets my time and attention. I admit that I roll my eyes when preachers say Christians shouldn't watch Netflix or Amazon Prime etc., but perhaps I need to embrace a level of challenge on this issue? If I know more about the cast of *Grey's Anatomy* than I know about the heroes of faith in the Bible then maybe I do need to re-evaluate my use of time? It may be a nice bit of escapism to decide who I think McDreamy or McSteamy will end up dating next, but it doesn't exactly help me in times of crisis! It's like so much of life, finding a good balance. I want to build a life on a solid foundation, which means ensuring I am working on these important spiritual disciplines. If I do so, I will have the ability to face the storms of life with courage and hope that goes beyond natural logic, like Esther and Gwen.

REFLECTION

What inspires you the most about Esther's story? How can you apply this to your own situation?

Are you currently spending time praying and fasting about your situation? If not, could you begin to do so even if in a small way like I did – missing one meal a week, or committing to praying for ten minutes a day?

If you don't already, why not begin a prayer journal – my husband and I did during our challenge and we prayed for other people too. It's great to have a record of this and to revisit it and see what God has done.

Do you think there's a link between being strong on the spiritual disciplines and having an ability to be brave in the face of a crisis?

Do you have more of a preference for McDreamy or McSteamy? I wasn't a fan of either – my fave was actually Dr Riggs who now plays Jack in *Virgin River*.

PRAYER

God, the story of Esther is incredibly challenging and really prompts me to examine my own levels of faith. I'm so impressed by her trust in you, her bravery, and her willingness to walk in faith rather than sit in fear, despite the very severe consequences she risked in doing so. I also thank you for the example of my lovely friend Gwen, who is going through a very tough time with grace, strength, humour and joy, because she is grounded in you. I want to get my spiritual life in order, to make sure I am disciplined in reading your word, praying, fasting and listening to you. I know in doing so I will be much better equipped to deal with the trials I come up against. Help me to evaluate my use of time. I want to ensure that I prioritise my relationship with you. Amen.

GOD'S 'BUT' CAN BE OUTRAGEOUS

Elijah said to her, 'Don't be afraid. Go home and do as you have said. *But* first make a small loaf of bread for me from what you have and bring it to me, and then make something for yourself and your son.' (1 Kings 17:13)

At times, as in the verse above, God's 'but in' demands outrageous acts of faith on our part. Sometimes God asks us to do things that may well make us look stupid if they don't work out. We risk losing face, feeling embarrassed, looking like the cheese has slid off our cracker. Take a leaf out of ark-building Noah's book – sometimes faith will make you look stupid, until it starts to rain.

This story from 1 Kings 17 we opened today with blows my mind. It makes no logical, human sense at all. A woman who has virtually nothing, and is simply trying to keep herself and her son alive, bumps into the prophet Elijah. His request to her, especially in her predicament, is outrageous and way beyond insensitive. She is gathering sticks to be able to cook her last *ever* meal for herself and her son, and Elijah shouts to her – 'Can you get me a drink please? Oh, and while you are at it get me a nice chunk of break too!' She replies honestly (and way more graciously to him than I would've done): 'I don't have any bread – all I have is a bit of flour and oil, tonight I'll use it to make food for me and my son and then we will eat it and die' (see 1 Kgs 17:12).

The prophet Elijah's response to this is probably the rudest, weirdest and most inappropriate thing anyone could say. The way I would've responded is in brackets:

> 'Don't be afraid *(Oh, thanks that's very helpful advice during a severe famine)*. Go home and do as you have said *(Thanks for your permission to do what I was going to do anyway, Elijah)*. But first make a small loaf of bread for me, and then make something for yourself and your son.' *(What???? Oh, right, yes! What a fantastic idea! I'll feed you first. How convenient that God's told you that you should be fed first! Jog on, you weirdo prophet. I'm scoffing the whole panini myself.)*

This widow was a single, Gentile woman who would have been among the most poor and needy, especially in a time of severe drought and famine. She had no hope – her plan was literally to eat a meal with her son and die.

Occasionally I believe God asks seemingly ridiculous things of us to see if we truly trust him. He sometimes requires us to act in obedience and faith before he 'buts in' with the breakthrough. When we choose to obey him and operate in faith before the miracle happens we demonstrate confidence and expectation in God. Like the widow in this story we can give the last of our meagre resources to him and trust him to do the impossible with them.

If you have little hope today, give what little hope you do have to him.

If you are lacking in faith, give the scraps of faith you do have to him.

Maybe it means you make a donation when you are believing for a change in your own difficult financial situation (however, please do not give money to anyone with a weird name and/or haircut who says you'll be healed and have your own private jet in the next ten minutes if you send them three grand – there's plenty of this ilk around, unfortunately). If you are in a challenging time financially, please ask for wisdom from a mature Christian friend on the donation suggestion.

If you have little positivity, begin to change the words you are speaking, even just a little – decide to say at least one faith-filled Scripture a day out loud over your situation. Remember the story of the boy with the five loaves and two fishes? He willingly gave the little he had to Jesus and it was multiplied by the bucketful. Start somewhere and start small if you need to.

Maybe there's a physical act you can do in faith, before you get your breakthrough. For example, before we adopted our daughter, we felt strongly that God was leading us to adopt a girl with Down Syndrome, which we knew was very specific. We were told by professionals involved that it was unlikely that we would adopt a child with Down Syndrome. We were regularly encouraged to widen our search. But we held to our convictions as we felt strongly that God was leading us to adopt a child with Down Syndrome and also specifically a girl. So in faith we decorated her bedroom before there was any sign of her. I would stand in her room and pray for her, believing she was on the way. Not because I was dreaming it up out of thin air – I don't believe if I stand in my living room declaring God will give me a million quid and a date with Daniel Craig totally believing in faith then it will happen. No! (Sad times.) But we were confident that's what God had said to us. We hung onto that belief in faith and practically did an act of faith in preparing the room for the promise – our miracle girl – before she had even been born.

Look at verse 16 of our Elijah passage – it says that the jar of flour was not emptied and the jug of oil did not run dry 'in keeping with the word of the LORD spoken by Elijah.' *In keeping with the word of the Lord*. That's the important bit. If we are believing for something that's in keeping with the word of the Lord, we can be confident that regardless of how outrageous it seems to speak and act in faith, God will 'but in' for us and bless us abundantly for our obedience.

God required an outrageous act of faith on the widow's part. To trust God with the very last of her human resources, and to trust him to turn them into more than enough. The miracle came after her act of obedience.

REFLECTION

What could be your 'But first' act
of obedience? I'm definitely not
suggesting you sell all of your
worldly possessions and jump on the
next boat to outer Mongolia as an
outrageous act of faith. But I am encouraging you to
begin to build your faith muscles. Start to flex your
spiritual pecs (Er, OK, maybe not, we'll stick with building
faith muscles. I don't want to encourage the wiggling of
pecs, whether they be spiritual or physical).

Start small – with a small act of faith in your situation.
Speak out a Scripture, sing a faith-filled song, speak words
of life. You can build up to outrageous prophet-bread-steal-
ing levels of faith! Give what you have to God in faith and
watch him do extraordinary things with it.

Ask God about what could be your 'but first' small act of
obedience today.

PRAYER

God, I acknowledge today that you sometimes require acts of obedience where we risk losing face, before you 'but in' with a miracle. The level of faith the widow displayed in today's passage is incredible. She was willing to give the little she had, the last of her worldly resources, to you. You did an incredible miracle, and as she gave what she had to you, you caused it to never run out. I thank you today for another faith-raising miracle. I remind myself again that you are Almighty God and nothing is impossible for you. Today, I am open to you challenging me to take a step of obedience. Show me a way I can step out in faith and use the little I have as an offering of trust in you. Amen.

GOD'S 'BUT' READS THE ROOM

Then the high priest stood up and said to Jesus, 'Are you not going to answer? What is this testimony that these men are bringing against you?' *But* **Jesus remained silent.**
(Matthew 26:62–3)

I believe it's really important to develop the gift of discernment in terms of knowing how to act and respond in times of difficulty. Often in such situations our emotions are so heightened that it can be difficult to operate in wisdom and with a sense of calmness and confidence. When situations make us feel threatened, depressed or victimised we can respond by trying our best to defend ourselves. We can go on the offensive.

Personally, from our situation – when we were told it was very unlikely to happen for us – I did a lot of research. I spoke to several relevant organisations for their professional perspectives and it was helpful to take action and get informed. We were given the opportunity to make a statement to the people making the decision on our situation. In all honesty I was ready with all of my research and information to write something that strongly supported us moving forward. However, when it came down to it I just didn't have peace about doing that. God clearly dropped into my mind this

Scripture from today about Jesus remaining silent when he was on trial. Jesus had a calm assurance that he was in the will of God. He knew who he was and whose he was. He didn't need to rant and debate and prove them wrong, which he could have done in a heartbeat, completely wiping the floor with them.

I shared with my husband that I felt like we needed to keep our statement very brief and I shared with him that I was reminded of the 'Jesus remaining silent' Scripture. He said he knew that's what I was going to say as God had reminded him of that too. We agreed that despite the fact that we were armed with positive evidence to 'but in' and support ourselves in our situation, we should choose not to go in with all guns blazing.

We also felt that by leaving out all of the supportive info, we raised the stakes in terms of faith. Without us backing our case with evidence, we felt it involved more faith to trust in God's ability to turn this around – but not as a result of any persuasion from us. If we did get a positive outcome we would know it was totally God and not due to us.

I'm not advocating for people in every situation to follow this silent protocol! Ecclesiastes 3:7 says there's a time to talk and a time to be silent – both speaking up and remaining silent are necessary at different times. It may be that in your situation you do need to speak up. My point today is that we need to be discerning and 'read the room' of our situation.

I think you'll know which is appropriate as you'll have peace about that decision. I knew that it wasn't right to pipe up in our situation. I was very vocal in other ways, as I've shared before, in terms of praying out loud God's promises and his word, singing songs of praise and victory. But I knew from spiritually 'reading the room' in our situation that our response needed to be one of silent confidence. I didn't need to strive, argue or 'but in' and prove my point in this particular scenario.

I love this Scripture from Psalm 57:2–3:

> I cry out to God Most High,
>   to God who vindicates me.
> He sends from heaven and saves me,
>   rebuking those who hotly pursue me –
>   God sends forth his love and his faithfulness.

It goes on to say:

> They dug a pit in my path –
>   but they have fallen into it themselves.
> My heart, O God, is steadfast.

The word 'vindicate' means 'provide justification or defence for', 'set free', 'deliver', 'defend'. There are some occasions when we do not need to vindicate ourselves, we need to trust God to do that. I knew that was true for me in our specific situation, and having the discernment to know that was so important.

How great is the verse from Psalm 57 where David's enemy digs a pit and then falls in it themselves? This is what God can do – he can provide this level of protection, victory and vindication in our impossible situations. Having a steadfast heart and a stead-fast confidence in God means we don't need to defend our corner every time because we know God is acting on our behalf. Isaiah 64:4 says that God 'acts on behalf of those who wait for him'. Waiting and trusting in God to 'but in' is not passive, it's an act of faith that he truly is in control.

We need to spiritually 'read the room' and discern God's leading in our particular situation.

REFLECTION

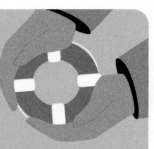

Are you striving, on the offensive? How would you feel if God asked you to stop with the evidence and proof and let him take care of it?

Do you feel you are in a time of needing to speak up or be silent?

Spend some time in prayer, asking God to give you wisdom to read the room of your own personal situation.

PRAYER

God, today I ask for your wisdom in my specific challenging situation. Please help me to read the room and give me the spiritual discernment that I need to do so. I want to deal with this in a godly way, and in a way that is emotionally mature. Thank you for the example of Jesus who knew when to speak up and when to be silent. Thank you that you vindicate me and you can deal with my enemies, so I don't need to be on the offensive and fight my own corner. Give me a steadfast heart that is at rest in you. I choose today not to strive, but to listen to you for wisdom in reading the room and responding well to my circumstances. Amen.

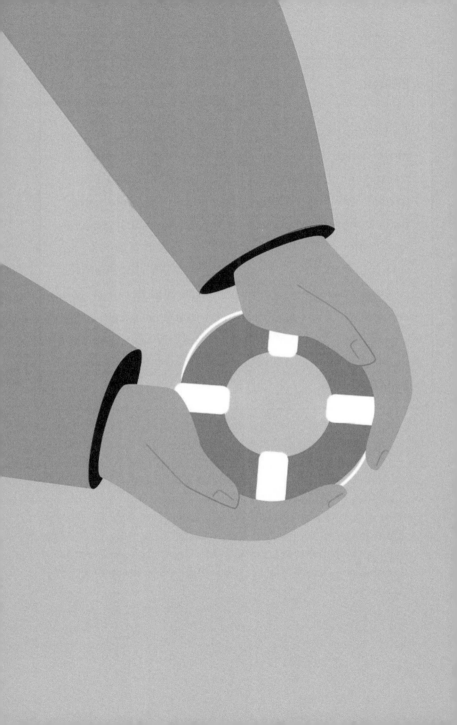

GOD'S 'BUT' CHECKS THE MAIL

You yourselves are our letter, written on our hearts, known and read by everyone. You show that you are a letter from Christ, the result of our ministry, written not with ink *but* with the Spirit of the living God, not on tablets of stone but on tablets of human hearts. (2 Corinthians 3:2–3)

In the Apostle Paul's day, letters of recommendation were given to new groups of believers to state that a teacher was approved of and commended by others. In 1 Corinthians 3, Paul argues that such letters of recommendation are unnecessary – his reason for this is his view that the Corinthian believers are themselves 'living letters'. Instead of letters written in ink, people should be able to look at the lives of Christians and be able to 'read' the letter of their life. Their faith, love, credibility, genuineness, hope, joy – and more – should clearly be communicated in their words and deeds. As believers I think we should aim to be 'the post with the most' or 'a living letter that makes life better'. (Side note – 'post' means 'mail' in the UK – if you are from elsewhere and reading this you could replace 'the post with the most' with 'the mail that doesn't fail' if you so wish).

Today I want us to consider our role in the world as God's living letters, and the responsibility we carry. How would you answer the question: 'In your current situation of difficulty and challenge, as you wait in faith for God to "but in", what is the letter of your life communicating to those around you?'

My husband and I love the arrival of the post each day. It's sad and shows that we are getting very old but it's true nevertheless! We have found that there are two different categories of post. It's rare, but it's a very good day when one of us receives 'exciting post'. Examples of 'exciting' post for me would include an unexpected handwritten card, or a parcel I've been keenly waiting for. The most recent parcel I received also shows that I'm ageing rapidly as it was a selection of modesty panels in an array of colours to protect the world from 'cleavage o'clock'. And all of the church modesty police said in unison, 'Amen'! The other type of post is 'rubbish post', which consists of boring bills, random leaflets about blinds or, even worse – speeding tickets (current tally – Husband: 4; Kate: 0).

Whether you receive exciting or rubbish post, both have an impact on your day. Exciting post brings life and a little lift as it's delivered. Rubbish post can bring groans, misery or even anxiety and dread. As a living letter yourself, what do you bring as you are delivered to the lives of others? Does your arrival into your home/workplace/gym/pub/local shop bring life, love, credibility, authenticity and joy? Or do you rock up somewhere carrying a gloomy, complaining, negative presence? Are you more royal mail or royal fail?!

As we are walking through challenging times and believing in God for a miracle, we need to maintain a strong awareness that we are 'living letters'. It's very easy to become self-focused when we are desperate for God to change something big in our lives.

It can become all-consuming. We need to be determined that whatever we are facing, we will bring life to others and represent Jesus well. When people are in the middle of a challenge yet are still able to bring joy, peace and kindness to the lives of others, it's an incredible witness to the goodness of God. Your letter doesn't need to be a false and sickly sweet love letter if that's not how you are feeling. Your letter needs to be honest and authentic, carrying the tension of your challenge and your belief in God to 'but in' and change things. Your 'living letter life' also needs to be mindful of the needs and feelings of others around you who are likely to be experiencing their own challenges.

The delivery of the letter of your life is also of great importance. We have a fantastic postwoman who goes the extra mile to ensure our post gets to us safely. If we miss a parcel and she later sees our car in the drive she will try again so we don't miss the delivery. Deliveries with other companies are not always as efficient; they are not as carefully and consistently conducted as the Royal Mail ones are. We've had parcels abandoned all day on our doorstep, or flung over the back gate in the middle of winter snow. Snow thanks.

This devotional has focused a lot on faith, and on hanging on in the belief that God will 'but in' and bring a breakthrough in our circumstances. Faith in bleak situations is vital and it really is a kingdom mindset that doesn't make logical sense. I really want to cultivate the mountain-moving levels of faith we have examined throughout this book. What's really important to note, though, is that above all we must do our best to walk in love. I read a Scripture last night that really brought this home to me. It's from 1 Corinthians 13:2 and it says: 'If I have a faith that can move mountains, but do not have love, I am nothing.' Wow, strong words. I feel this ties in really well with today's thoughts on us being living letters. We can be God's love letters to the people we meet, bringing his love, life and hope. Love is everything. Resolve to spread some 'first class' love wherever you go! What a great privilege and responsibility we have as God's 'letters on legs'!

As living letters, we also need to deliver the message of our living letters kindly and considerately – Royal Mail-style. During a testing time in life, the temptation can be to dramatically hurl ourselves over the gate and cause damage with our delivery. I am trying (though not always succeeding) to erase the drama and stress I can bring along with the letter of my life due to the challenge I'm facing. Let's be determined to represent Jesus well with both the delivery and content of the letters of our lives.

Yours sincerely,
K. Williams

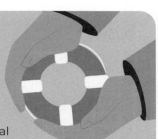

REFLECTION

How does knowing that you are a 'living letter' make you feel?

Do you think you've been more Royal Mail or royal fail in regards to the delivery of the letter of your life?

How can you live out your living letter with authenticity and bringing glory to God, despite being in a very testing time?

How does the Scripture 'If I have not love, I am nothing' make you feel?

Do you like thinking of yourself as one of God's 'letters on legs?' I really dislike my legs as they are really short, Ronnie Corbett-length legs, so viewing myself as God's 'letter on legs' helps me to walk taller (spiritually if not physically speaking)!

PRAYER

God, I really want to be a living letter that is authentic and I want the letter of my life to bring joy, hope, authenticity and peace to others. I want to make sure that the delivery of my living-letter life is gentle, thoughtful and life-giving. I don't want to deliver the letter of my life in a harsh, negative way that brings others down. Help me to be mindful that your word says that my living letter is 'known and read by everyone' and I have a responsibility to reflect you well to the watching world. Thank you that my letter doesn't have to paint a fake picture that everything is rosy. I can be honest and real, but help me to always include words of hope and faith regardless of my situation. Amen.

GOD'S 'BUT' DANCES WITH JOY

Weeping may stay for the night *but* rejoicing comes in the morning. (Psalm 30:5)

This week we will receive our decision on whether we can go forward and become foster carers. After reflecting on these biblical 'but ins' I'm genuinely in a place of peace, faith and expectation that we will get approved. My faith has certainly been tested but it has also grown. I have experienced a lot of discouragement and disappointment on a human level, but also a lot of encouragement and strength from God, his word, and the amazing people supporting us. I'm a weird mixture of drained, knackered, hopeful and excited all at the same time. For the first time in my Christian life, I'm in a place where I honestly believe God not only can but will do this. He spoke so clearly at a point of real crisis in the process we are in, and his word brought peace, relief, faith and confidence. He can be trusted, and we must live by his words and not our circumstances.

I'm writing this final 'but' from a coffee shop opposite the organisation who are making the final decision for us this week. I'm seeing this as a statement of faith and 'claiming ground' rather than a creepy stalker-type thing to do! Let's hope I'm not showing up on their CCTV. I'm not going full on, Jericho-style marching around seven times hollering with trumpets (although I did play a kazoo for the first time over the weekend so I'd be well equipped!). I'm sitting here, looking at the building, thinking about how I'll soon be going in there for meetings and training, and I'm praying I will have a positive impact there. I believe as a result of this dream being fulfilled, I will live out the calling God has placed upon me, and while I sit here, I'm praying that I will bless and help others as I do so.

This final 'but' is an important one, and one we must try to remember during challenging times. Weeping and hard times do certainly hit our lives. Not every day is a barrel of laughs, fun and winning. But God's word states that while we may go through a time of weeping, there is joy coming. You may feel like you'll never feel joyful again because what you are facing is so hard. A few weeks back I felt like my life was crumbling – it felt like one difficult conversation after another and not much hope at all. But I believe God's word is true, and that you and me will indeed have joyful times ahead. If you are in a time of mourning, weeping and difficulty, process it and take time to walk through it, but hold on to hope that joy is coming. Ecclesiastes 3:4 says there's a time to cry, to laugh, to dance and to mourn. We go through different 'seasons' in life and, like the natural seasons, they do shift.

Later in Psalm 30, David says:

> You turned my wailing into dancing;
>> you removed my sackcloth and clothed me with joy. (v. 11)

I'm believing that sometime this week I will be dancing round my lounge after receiving the news that we can go ahead. It's been a long and difficult season, but I can see the sun finally making its way over the horizon. God's 'but' can turn my mourning into dancing, and my butt gladly accepts the invitation to dance with joy and celebration when the good news comes.

Wherever you find yourself at the point of reading this, I pray that you will have the ability to hold on to hope, believe in faith for a miracle, and look forward to your dancing days ahead. I'd encourage you to live with a strong awareness of God's ability to 'but in', because God's 'but' really can change everything.

REFLECTION

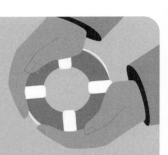

As you look back on your life so far, can you remember times when everything felt so dark that you thought you'd never feel joy again?

Do you believe that God will one day change your situation around and, like with David, he will turn your mourning into dancing?

Do you find the analogy of the changing seasons that happen in nature helpful in believing your situation will change?

Type 'Seasons – Hillsong' into YouTube and reflect on the beautiful lyrics. There are serious Christmas vibes, but this song really helped me and I pray it speaks to you too.

PRAYER

God, I'm encouraged to remember today that although we walk through many different trials and tests, you promise us that we will again experience your joy. I think of the natural seasons, and it gives me hope that spiritually speaking this wintery season will shift and I will enjoy some spring and summer times ahead. Weeping and mourning are part of our human experience, but so are joy and celebration. I remind myself today that you say, 'Weeping may last for the night, but joy comes in the morning'. I look forward to experiencing joy again and trust you that this will happen, as unlikely as that may feel right now. Amen.

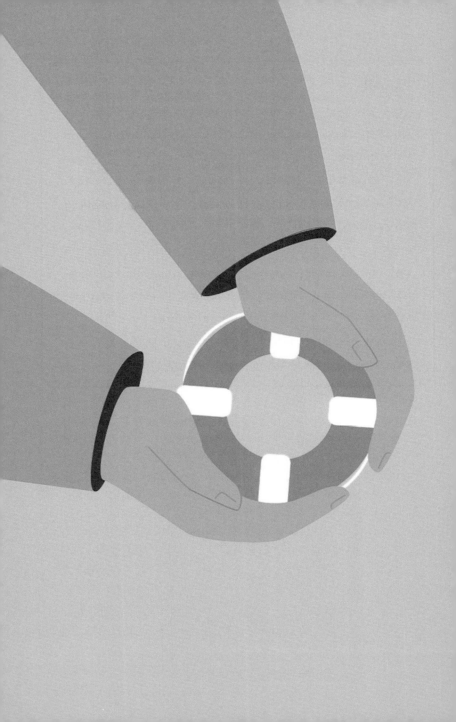

EPILOGUE – *BUT* WHAT HAPPENED NEXT?

I felt like I wanted to end by filling you in on what happened in my impossible situation, and I hope it stirs faith, hope and also perhaps an 'embracing of mystery' in you as you read what comes next.

We were given the green light to proceed with our dream to become foster carers – it was definitely a case of God doing 'more than we could ask, think or imagine' (Eph. 3:20) in how he made a way! I can only describe it as God did it all and put a cherry on the top (probably not the best analogy as if I have a cake with a cherry on top I pick off said cherry pronto and flick it at someone I'm not keen on). I honestly believe God did a miracle, as the turnaround in our situation was amazing. We had been advised to back out of the process as we were 'highly unlikely' to be approved, but in October 2019 we were given the good news that we were fully approved – and our approval was even extended to include short-term foster care as well as the respite care we had applied to do.

We were active in providing respite care, almost straight away. We supported a young girl for a full weekend as a one-off arrangement. We then went on to support a young man aged 11 once a month for nearly a year. The times he came to stay with us went really well. We got to watch a lot of Marvel films accompanied by pepperoni pizza, which made a welcome change from Peppa Pig and chicken nuggets! He got on well with our daughter, which really helped; he was very kind and nurturing towards her. It was a privilege to support him, and also lovely for us to know that his main foster carers were enjoying a nice peaceful meal out or night away while he was with us. We know this made a real difference to them. Our placement with him was a temporary one. It was planned to just be for during the Covid pandemic, but we were hopeful that another placement would happen soon after.

We had a couple of positive-sounding opportunities that in the end just didn't come off. For the last eight months we've been working towards a placement to support a little girl each month but it all fell through just a few weeks ago. As I write this epilogue it's now November 2022 and almost eighteen months have passed since we've had a placement. I felt like sharing this with you, as I want to be real about how much mystery and confusion we can experience even after God does a significant miracle, and I want to tell you how I'm dealing with that.

In honesty, I have at times felt bombarded by disappointment and confusion. Despite the fact that for a year we were active in our dream, it hasn't been at all what I had hoped or longed for it to be. We have definitely done good and blessed people and it has been a positive experience overall, but it's not been the fulfilment of what I felt God had originally put on my heart many years ago when the dream of fostering began to grow. I believed God would extend our family to include another little person via fostering.

I feel confused and disheartened about why God would have given me such specific Scriptures, and make a way so miraculously, for us to experience so few results. I have tied myself in knots questioning why God would move a mountain for my dream not to be fulfilled in the way I had so eagerly longed for.

Two people have helped me in my struggle with these questions. One is Danielle Strickland, and the other is Brennan Manning (who I keep mistakenly referring to as either Bernard Manning or Bernard Matthews!). Brennan Manning (not an old comedian or a seller of poultry) wrote a great book called *The Ragamuffin*

Gospel. I thank God for wise people like Brennan and Danielle who we can look to during times of difficulty.

So often, if I've felt confused in life, people have said to me something along the lines of, 'God is the author of peace, he doesn't want you to be confused.' I totally get where they are coming from and up until recently, I pretty much agreed with them. Then I read something Danielle Strickland said, which has begun to shift my thinking somewhat: 'Embrace the posture of confused and disturbed as a lifestyle because that's what it feels like to be called by God. We resist those places because "it can't be God" to feel this way, but if you read your Bibles, you'll see how often it actually is.' She goes on to say:

> There is a peace that passes all understanding that can be given by God and received by us. But it is not a peace like the world gives – it is an eternal assurance that no matter what, God is with us. The reason we need this is because much of the time we can't quite figure out how this kingdom business is gonna work out! Most of the time it looks helpless and we feel weak. Confused and disturbed, we are still invited to receive peace through the endless and unlimited presence of God . . . The more confusing the more opportunity to trust God.[3]

I have found this to be so helpful. I want (and expect) that as a Christian, God will speak to me, direct me and I'll know his leading. While this is true and he absolutely does do those things, there are still times when we feel he is silent and we do feel totally confused.

This was not uncommon to the believers we read of in the Bible. Imagine how it must have felt when Jesus died. They'd spent time living and travelling with him, getting to know him, being loved and discipled by him and then suddenly he's gone. He is then resurrected and hope returns, until he leaves yet again as he ascends back to heaven. They then have a time of waiting for the Holy Spirit to come upon them. It's such a mix of uncertainty, wonder, confusion, hope, faith, excitement and despair. Why do I then expect that my life as a believer will be one easy step after another, always feeling totally confident that I know what God is saying and never ever experiencing confusion and uncertainty?

I'm learning that times like these can lead to greater levels of trust. The one thing I have prayed for over this specific fostering situation during the last three years has been clarity. God, please give me clarity. I had such clarity when we adopted our daughter – such a specific promise from God about a child with Down Syndrome. But now I'm just totally confused, I don't know what God is doing – he has spoken so specifically to me before and now he's pretty silent. I just want CLARITY PLEASE!

I recently listened to a sermon called 'The Way of Trust' by Brennan Manning. He said that clarity can actually be the enemy of trust. He quotes Mother Teresa, who was asked to pray for clarity for someone and she refused saying: 'I will not do that. Clarity is the last thing you are clinging to and you've got to let go of it. I will pray that you will *trust*.' Brennan says, 'In craving clarity, we seek to avoid the risk of trust.' That hit home with me. I know my personality is one of liking control, planning, to know what's happening and when so I can be well prepared. Nothing terribly wrong with that, in fact those things can be a great strength. But they don't always work so well in my spiritual life, at times when God doesn't share the specifics of his plans with me. When he doesn't give the clarity I'm pleading for, and I have to remain in the dark. However, I'm learning that dark, confusing times like these are a real opportunity for trust. I recognise that in this situation I need to stop asking for clarity, and to start to ask God to help me submit to his plans and his schedule. To learn 'the way of trust' so that, even if I don't ever see the fulfilment of this dream that I had so longed for,

I still accept that he has reasons for leading us on this journey that I may never know or understand.

On reflection, I can see that throughout this experience I have done a lot of learning. I've recently read a lot about how we all have limitations, and how these limitations can actually be a gift to us. Caring for another child, even just once a month, did in honesty really stretch us as a family. Our daughter has not slept well for the last couple of years and this is a very real limitation we are facing as it greatly diminishes our energy levels and abilities to function well. I have learnt that I need to stop looking at how much other people are doing and feeling like a failure in comparison. We have friends who have three, four, five, even six children and they also have jobs, hobbies and still manage to be quite nice people! I have to recognise that I do not have the capacity for all of that – especially the being nice part! But it's not because I'm rubbish compared to them, it's because I have different assignments from God. I love writing – this whole fostering process caused me to write this devotional which I really pray will help people who read it. I also love sign language, and learning and perfecting this craft takes up a lot of time and dedication. We have to focus on what God is calling us personally to do, and recognise that we all have limitations and different capacities – none of us can do it all. Perhaps God in his kindness allowed me to do some fostering to recognise that I actually don't have the capacity to care for another vulnerable child as I had hoped I could.

We met with our social worker this week and it looks like our fostering journey will be coming to an end, at least for now – this felt like the right decision for both sides. I feel a mixture of sadness, frustration, peace and acceptance about this. It's not a permanently closed door by any means. We are able to revisit fostering through them at a later date if we wish to and they said they would be very supportive of this. We will continue to have a positive link with the organisation, and have talked about ways we can continue to support them in more of a voluntary capacity.

We have put a lot of practical and emotional energy into this fostering journey, and I have to admit that I'm wrestling with it feeling like a waste of time, or a lot of work for very little fruit. The hours we have spent in training, attending support groups and activities, plus the paperwork has been a lot. It doesn't really make sense to me. But we have prayed about it and released it to God as best as we can. I'm acknowledging that it's OK to feel grief as, at least for now, it's the loss of a dream. We have asked God to bring fostering back to us if it's supposed to happen in the future. I'm embracing this lesson of trusting God through foggy times. I'm determined that in my wrestling with this, I will keep trusting that God has had purposes in this that I may not fully understand.

I hope that though this is perhaps not a fairytale ending, it stirs your heart to keep going, to keep persevering and to keep believing for God to 'but in' for you. God certainly did something significant in our fostering approval. I would encourage you that wherever you are up to on your journey, you hold on for God's 'but in', and that you cling on tightly to him because he truly knows best and can absolutely be trusted.

The 'but' I'd like you to remember above all to continue to stir your faith is this one: 'Humanly speaking, it is impossible. BUT with God everything is possible' (Matt. 19:26). He really did do the impossible in our situation, and I encourage you to believe for the same in your impossible situation too.

Sending much love and prayers from my 'but' to your 'but',

Kate xx

ABOUT THE AUTHOR

Kate is in her happy place when she's writing in a coffee shop, with a one-shot latte (and earwigging in on other people's conversations – multitasking at its best). Kate is passionate about connecting with people through writing and speaking – sharing God's truth in a way that is honest and authentic, along with a sprinkling of humour and some truly terrible puns!

This is Kate's first book, but if you enjoyed it she has more writing projects in the pipeline – so keep an eye out!

If you'd like to follow Kate's writing updates please connect with her on Instagram @katewilliamswrites.

You can also contact Kate via email at katewilliamswriting@gmail.com.

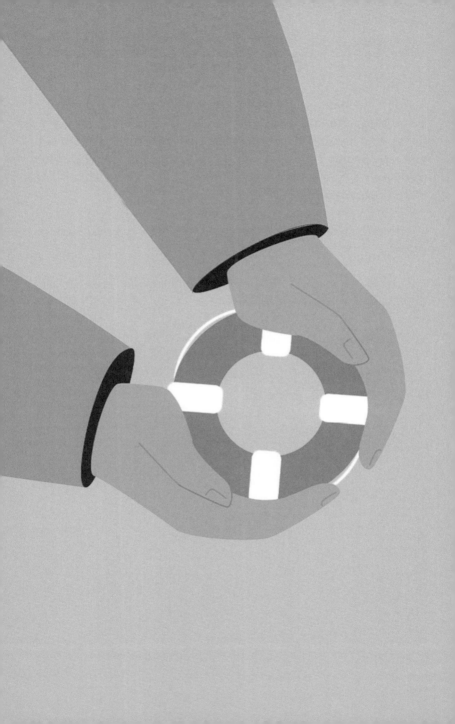

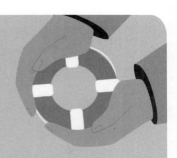

MY REFLECTIONS

MY REFLECTIONS

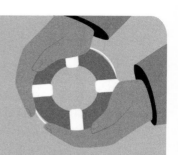

MY REFLECTIONS

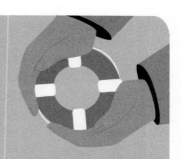

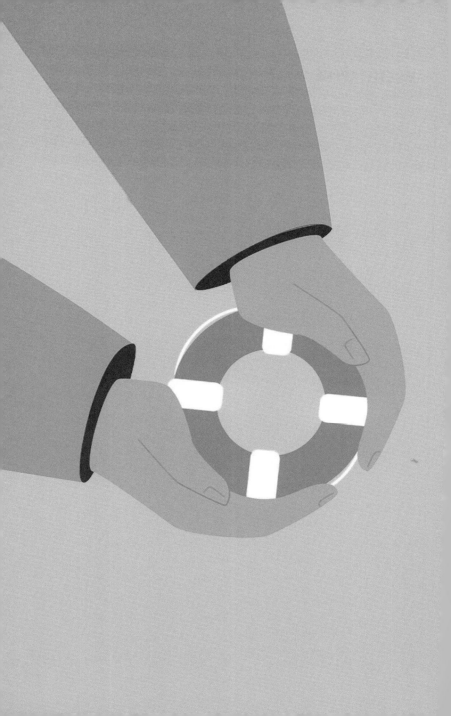

MY PRAYER

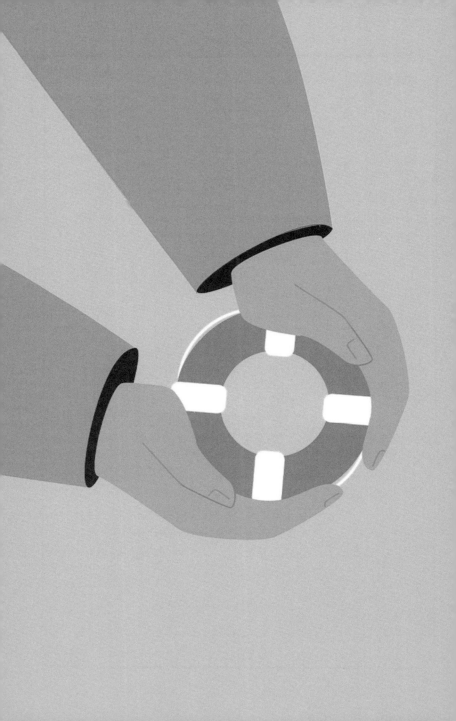

NOTES

1. Nate Johnson on Instagram, https://www.instagram.com/p/CEUSmRYJhP-/ (accessed 19 June 2023). Used by permission.
2. See *Daily Office: Remembering God's Presence throughout the Day* by Pete Scazzero (Barrington, IL: Willow Creek Association, 2008), pp. 40–57.
3. Danielle Strickland on Instagram, https://www.instagram.com/p/CQwCMTMjAB0/ (accessed 29 June 2023). Used by permission.

Say Goodbye to Anxiety

*A 40-day devotional journal to
overcome fear and worry*

Elle Limebear and Jane Kirby

Anxiety has been calling the shots for too long. Enough is enough, it's
time to say goodbye.

Elle and Jane get it. Having both suffered with anxiety, they understand how it can impact our daily lives. They also know the difference
Jesus can make.

As they honestly share their story, Elle and Jane support and cheer us
on as they offer God-given practical tools and strategies to overcome
anxiety.

Be encouraged, through these 40 devotional thoughts and journaling
reflections, to take daily steps with God's help to move past anxiety
and live life to the full.

978-1-78893-312-4

Be – Godly Wisdom to Live By

365 devotions for women

Fiona Castle and friends

Jesus gave us the greatest love of all. We are called not just to keep it to ourselves, but to overflow with that love to others. But how can we really do that in the busyness of our lives?

In these daily devotions, women from many walks of life share insights on scripture and practical life lessons to gently encourage you to live for Jesus, and to be more like him in your thoughts, character, and actions.

Discover godly wisdom that will help you navigate the world as a Christian woman and live out God's unique purpose for your life.

978-1-78893-239-4

Safe All Along

Trading our fears and anxieties for God's unshakable peace

Katie Davis Majors

As a missionary, wife, and mum of fifteen, Katie Davis Majors knows how hard it can be to receive God's peace instead of giving in to fear and worry. Family emergencies, unexpected life-shifting events, and the busy rhythms of family life have at times left her reeling.

In *Safe All Along,* Katie offers reflections and stories from around the world and from her own kitchen table about her personal journey toward living from a place of surrendered trust. Every chapter leads us deep into Scripture as we learn what it looks like to break free from anxiety and take hold of peace.

Our God has promised us a peace that transcends all understanding. And we can accept his promise, trusting that in him we are safe all along.

978-1-78893-316-2

With These Hands

*Holding on to God
in the storms of life*

Leanne Mallett

Leanne's battle with breast cancer forced her to face some of her greatest fears and tested her faith in a way she had never experienced before. Treatment changed her appearance and stripped her of her identity as a woman, and her life was changed.

With deep honesty, Leanne shares how she dealt with this new reality and reveals the lessons she learned about God's incredible faithfulness and the strength that he gives us when we need it most.

978-1-78893-274-5

Hope Wins

How a vision of our eternal future
impacts our lives today

Goff Hope

Hope is fundamental for human wellbeing but it is in short supply
in our world. We can quickly be robbed of hope by illness, personal
tragedy or by the sheer oppressive nature of news headlines.

Drawing on his own personal experiences, including the tragedy of
losing his daughter and his own battle with cancer, Goff shares how
holding on to the Christian hope of an eternal future transformed the
darkest moments of his life.

Interweaving personal testimony of the goodness of God with biblical
teaching on heaven, Goff encourages us to see that when tough times
come, and we are tempted to doubt or ask the big questions, such as
Why, Lord?, we can have hope if we keep our eyes on Jesus and have a
heavenly perspective on life.

978-1-78893-276-9

Salt Water and Honey

*Lost dreams, good grief,
and a better story*

Lizzie Lowrie

Reeling from the disappointment of a failed business venture, Lizzie Lowrie's life takes a nightmarish turn as she suffers miscarriage after miscarriage.

Written from the messy middle of life, where there are no neat or cliched answers, Lizzie honestly shares her pain and the fight to find God in her suffering.

Providing a safe space to remind people that they're not alone, it's okay to grieve and their story matters, this is for anyone who has lost their dream and is struggling to understand their purpose when life looks nothing like they hoped it would.

978-1-78893-095-6

Authentic

We trust you enjoyed reading this book from Authentic. If you want to be informed of any new titles from this author and other releases you can sign up to the Authentic newsletter by scanning below:

Online:
authenticmedia.co.uk

Follow us: